"WISE, WITTY, PRACTICAL, MORDANT, FUNNY,
this is the only guide to becoming a writer that may actually
work. It's a primer on Carolyn See: great artist, large soul."
—JAMES ELLROY

"Carolyn See doesn't just tell you to sharpen your pencils, she
shows you how to sharpen your wits."
—RITA MAE BROWN

"See brings the writer out of contemplative solitude and into
the marketplace. Here is a pep talk, a revved-up compendium
of suggestions and tricks (as if there could be any tricks that
are not at the very same time truthful insights) meant to help
the practitioner find success in what is all too often a
discouraging literary world."
—*Los Angeles Times Book Review*

"Perfect for the budding writer in the family, although, truly,
you'd have to be humor-impaired not to love this book. See,
a novelist and highly entertaining book critic, shares her advice
on writing and life in general with wry wit."
—*The Miami Herald*

"After reading *Making a Literary Life*, I have decided to
abandon my present career and become an aspirant writer,
this time guided by Carolyn See's wonderfully instructive
(and readable) book."
—WILLIAM F. BUCKLEY JR.

"Honest and true . . . See talks about character, plot, voice,
and point of view with genial wisdom and examples that don't
depend on a deep affinity for Henry James."
—*The Dallas Morning News*

Please turn the page for more reviews. . . .

Making a Literary Life

Advice for Writers and

Other Dreamers

Carolyn See

Ballantine Books / New York

A Ballantine Book
Published by The Random House Publishing Group

Copyright © 2002 by Carolyn See

All rights reserved under International and Pan-American Copyright Conventions.
Published in the United States by The Random House Publishing Group, a division
of Random House, Inc., New York, and simultaneously in Canada by Random
House of Canada Limited, Toronto.

Ballantine and colophon are registered trademarks of Random House, Inc.

www.ballantinebooks.com

Library of Congress Control Number: 2003094620

ISBN 0-345-44046-3

This edition published by arrangement with Random House, Inc.

Book design by J. K. Lambert
Cover design by Chin-Yee Lai

Manufactured in the United States of America

First Random House Hardcover Edition: August 2002
First Ballantine Books Trade Paperback Edition: September 2003

2   4   6   8   10   9   7   5   3   1

Contents

PART III: DURING, AND AFTER

Introduction

Making a Literary Life is not necessarily for the already successful and sophisticated. It's for students just coming to this discipline, older people who wanted to write in their youth and never got around to it, folks who live in parts of the country where the idea of writing is about as strange as crossbreeding a tomato and a trout.

This book is for the timid, forlorn, and clueless. It will tell you everything I know about how you can learn to write in your own voice, how, with some luck and work and play, you can achieve enough publication, reputation, and recognition to make you happy. More important—or *as* important, I believe— it will tell you everything I know about not butting your head futilely against what we might call everyday life. This is about making your own *literary* life, wherever you are, wherever you live, whoever your family and friends may be.

—

"Carolyn cares more about the writing life than she does about writing."

"Carolyn hasn't succeeded in breaking the boundaries of the pre-Joycean novel."

These two statements were made at one of those faculty promotion meetings where they make it an "ethical" point to pass on every mean thing anybody ever says about you without saying who said it. (It doesn't matter; I was already a full professor. And they were nice people, doing their best.)

They were partly right. There's never been a morning in my life when I catapulted out of bed and said, "Okay! This is it! Stand back, pre-Joycean novel! Today's the day those boundaries come a-tumblin' down!" It's true that I love to write, second only to how much I love my children, that I entertain the thought that if I'm good enough, what I write might change the world for the better. I love the life too; I loved overhearing the president of the Writers Guild asking the late Max Shulman, shyly, like a girl on a first date, "When do you write?" "In the morning, if I can," he answered. I love standing in line at book signings and having the sense, if there's no one behind me in the line, to blab on to the writer for twenty minutes so that the writer won't die. I love big literary fundraisers and drinking bad wine from a plastic glass or phoning my daughters to groan about publishing—because my daughters are writers, too.

But mostly, *of course,* I love sitting on the couch in my sweats, turning on Van Morrison just below audio level—I can hear him, but not really, inviting me to meet him down by the pylons or to listen to the lion or to not have a guru or a preacher—and then writing my thousand words: *my* thousand words, which have nothing to do with breaking the boundaries of the pre-Joycean novel and everything to do with what it means to be living right now, right here, in my particular place in America. Because I believe, with a patriotic sincerity that would make a Legionnaire blush, that American literature is owned by everybody in America and that world lit is owned by everyone in the world and that we all get to have a say in it, not just a comparatively few men and women in the Northeast, no matter how decent and talented they may be.

——

This book is divided into three parts, and is intended to cover the writing process from the first moment you decide, or dream, that you want to write, on through to the third month after publication of your first novel, when you get to think—with a lot of serious trembling—about whether or not you'd want to do it again, really devote your life to this writing, this life, your literature.

Part One advises you how to gear up, *discreetly*, for what it is you want to do. It exhorts you not to talk about how you want to be a writer, because that bores people to death. On the other hand, it asks you to look around for your own material: not Stephen King's or Paul Auster's but your own. Your treasure. And—why not pretend to be a writer: What would it be like if you could really *do* it? It reminds you to begin to hang out with people who wouldn't hate it if you really did try your hand at writing. And because the whole project sounds so iffy, even as I write this, it gives you some tips on practicing white magic to get what you want, or at least not sabotaging yourself in pathetic ways. It tells you (and how proud I am of this chapter!) how to deal with rejection as a process, to see it as a kind of courtship that keeps your mind engaged and your heart from being broken. It gives you some useful tips on how to behave when your first article or short story is published—so that you won't embarrass your family and friends. Because nobody and no one wants a writer-jerk in the family. Most important, Part One starts you on a discipline of a thousand words a day, five days a week, and one charming note written to someone in the literary world who makes your hands sweat—five days a week, for the rest of your life.

Part One, then, is a combination of writing and life strategies, a beginning. And it ends when you publish your first work, whether it's an article on dementia in whales (or Wales) or an obscure piece in a literary magazine or your grandma's recipe for beef Stroganoff.

Part Two has to do with writing—but not writing according to somebody else's rules! Nothing to do with Melville or the newly fashionable slave narratives or Hemingway or Fitzgerald (except to show, maybe, how they use certain devices). I won't harangue you about deconstruction or controlling images. After suffering through graduate school and reading more than my share of critical essays, I can only offer up Part Two as a checklist of things you may or may not want to think about in your work: character, of course; plot—I believe I've come up with something new about plot; point of view—I'm a bit fanatical about this. A dentist I knew once impetuously had sex with one of his patients on the floor of his waiting room, then reared up on his elbows and said, "You know, you really need to floss more." I think—I *know*—that point of view is the literary equivalent of flossing; if you've got flossing down pat, your teeth will live happily on into eternity with your shining bones. I talk about geography, time, and space—because one of my own personal curses has been getting my characters into the car and out of the car—and a few other things. It's just a checklist, not an instruction book. The last thing in the world I want is to "teach you how to write." You already know how to write, even if you don't know that you know. And I include a useful chapter on rewriting.

You'll notice that I ask you again to write one "charming note" a day to a writer, editor, or agent *without asking a favor*—merely to express admiration and, when appropriate, love. These are paper airplanes of affection. They are the glue of human sweetness in literary society. What our mothers told us (if we were well brought up) is true: Manners and civility count for everything. Even if we're writing in a gutter, we can pull ourselves out long enough to write some charming notes (to take us from *this* world, where we're unhappy, to that other world, where we want to be).

Part Three begins at about the time you publish your first book, which is not as hard as it seems (the second one is the real trial), and takes a look at the fact that a "real" literary life may indeed be possible for you.

It's just another part of our demented fantasy that once we write the book, we are done with it; we can sit and think for a while and then go on to write another one. In reality, publication demands an almost Janus-faced split in your personality three months before and three months after your publication date. You hire a public-relations person or become one; you plan more parties than a cruise director. You realize (sometimes bitterly, sometimes philosophically) that your little book is only one of twenty or thirty that are being released by your publishing house that season and that *you're* the one, finally, responsible for the relative success or failure of your work. (That goes for your whole career, too.)

So Part Three deals with how to manage that first major publication, how to get up your courage to go to New York (a little like how Dorothy got to Oz, with advice on how to avoid some of those winged monkeys—or befriend them and take them out for a drink). Then there's always the sticky matter of making money as a writer—when and if you should ever quit your day job. And there's a final chapter on what it might mean if you ever get this far and deciding if the literary life is really what you want or need. The bigger the yacht, the more barnacles there are under the waterline. You can have this life, but do you want to spend a lot of it prying off barnacles?

—

To shorten explanations—and because that's the way I write, I guess—I'll be using a small cast of illustrative characters: each one is a fully complex and lovable creature in real life, but they are all reduced to allegorical characters here.

My ma, a tough customer with a dark view of life.

My old Texan dad, full of aphorisms, knowledge, charm, and concealed sorrow. A failed writer until he turned sixty-nine.

Lisa, my beautiful and accomplished older daughter, author of four books, who recognized her material early and is now becoming not just a household name but a Chinese-American legend.

Clara, my beautiful and accomplished younger daughter,

who works with homeless folks and is now an intrepid journalist fighting for justice.

Richard, Lisa's father, my first husband; handsome, funny, self-defined as a "failed" writer.

Tom, Clara's dad, darling, with the shortest fuse in Christendom; self-defined as a "failed" writer.

John Espey, distinguished scholar, my life partner for twenty-seven years; a wonderful, funny, "successful" writer.

Dash, my baby grandson, reincarnation of the sun god Ra.

Penny. That's me, in an earlier life; a "failed" writer with a tremendous chip on my shoulder.

These nine characters turn up from time to time—not because they're from *my* family, but because they represent *all* families, the people we have to deal with when we think about pursuing our dreams without making the lives of our friends and family—and our own—a living hell.

There are also a few figures of speech I'll be using—things I talk about in class or old jokes in our family that seem to cover a lot of ground.

THE RATS AND THE VITAMIN C EXPERIMENT

Some scientists (this is true) once got a few rats and two tubs of water together. They gave one set of rats massive doses of vitamin C and set them to swimming in one tub. The second set of rats got dumped unceremoniously into the other tub. The rats swam vigorously for twenty-four hours or so; then the second set of rats got tired and drowned. The vitamin C rats, however, went on swimming and swimming for so long that the scientists in the experiment got fed up with the project and fished the rats out—perky and refreshed from their bracing swim. Sometimes, in the writing/publishing process, it may cross your mind that the people in charge haven't been giving you the vitamin C, but that's when it's time to marshal your reserves and keep on swimming.

THE BIG-ADVANCE TRUFFLE PIG

An acquaintance of mine was writing a brilliant but fairly inaccessible book and looking for a publisher. I recommended a university press. Her husband told me, a little stiffly, "She's looking for a big advance." It made me laugh, and I told some of my friends about it. One, a hardworking journalist, said, "What she needs is a truffle pig—a big-advance truffle pig." It cheered us up, during the hard days that writers sometimes have, imagining that we each had our big-advance truffle pig out there snorting through the publishing underbrush. Who knows? They might come up with something!

MY OLD TEXAN DAD'S 18-HOUR CHILI, AND HIS 18-MINUTE CHILI

He was quite the cook! His recipe for Polynesian pork chops took six weeks to make. His 18-hour chili was labor-intensive: To do it right took everything out of him, and everybody around him. When it was finished, it was a masterpiece! People came from miles around to taste it, and tears came to their eyes. But life has its other requirements, and there were nights when he threw together his 18-minute chili. It tasted just fine and was far better than no chili at all. Most of our life falls somewhere in the middle. At the end of this introduction, I include my 18-hour and 18-minute chili rules for making a successful literary life. The thing to remember is that 18-minute chili is far better than no chili at all.

DATING / ONE-NIGHT STANDS / LOVE / SEX / COSMIC UNION

Aside from the actual writing—which might come under the heading of "solitary pleasure" or cosmic union with the entire universe—the publication process, a good part of the writing business, and the writing life can be alarmingly similar to romance, seduction, falling in love, having sex, getting a divorce, and falling in love again. It's a useful metaphor.

———

Making a Literary Life pertains, I think, to "serious" fiction, popular fiction, short stories, magazine pieces (you'd be surprised how much Mary Murphy at *TV Guide* and James Joyce have in common), serious nonfiction, popular nonfiction, essays, even, perhaps, some screenwriting. I don't think it works for scholarship or poetry.

Again, this book is for people all over the country who find themselves isolated from what we might customarily think of as the literary loop. The Out Crowd, if you like.

I may be idealistic, but I'm not crazy. The 18-minute-chili method can start you writing. The 18-hour-chili method, followed with joy, fun, and a degree of obsession, can change your life to a literary one.

P.S. I include a very short reading list at the back, both to illustrate some of the things I'm talking about and to remind you of the incredible diversity of the English language. Also, there are a few life-changing books included, works you'd be well advised to read before you die.

CAROLYN'S 18-MINUTE CHILI
"FUN FIRST!"

1. A thousand words a day—or two hours of revision—five days a week for the rest of your life.
2. A "charming note" (that does *not* ask for a favor) to a writer, editor, or agent you admire—five days a week for the rest of your life (or flowers, lunch, drinks, a helium balloon, etc.).

CAROLYN'S 18-HOUR CHILI
"FUN FIRST!"

1. A thousand words a day—or two hours of revision—five days a week for the rest of your life.
2. A "charming note" (that does *not* ask for a favor) to a writer, editor, or agent you admire—five days a week for the rest of your life (or flowers, lunch, drinks, a helium balloon, etc.).
3. An outside excursion once a week to a writing class or a conference or a book signing, where you buy a book from a live author.

4. Start where you are: What's the genre of your life? Opera, soap opera, action-adventure, cooking, erotica, screwball comedy? Don't lie to yourself. Really think!

5. Pretend—in your mind—to be a writer: "If I were a writer, what would I be like? What would I do? Where would I go?" Then think about how you can do it.

6. Make lists of what a writer "like you" might want: A personal assistant? An agent? A limo? A sympathetic lover? An entourage? Fame? Fortune? Respect? Snapshots of you and your friends living the good life in the south of France? A talk with God?

7. Try a little white magic—a few affirmations, visualizations, treasure maps (or, at the very least, avoid hexing yourself!).

8. Make rejection a process. Writing should be a courtship, not a charnel house! Befriend your enemies. Don't lose your temper! You're the seducer, and you *always* succeed.

9. Remember, it's a game. The objects are love, fun, and truth. If, on any given day, you've written your one thousand words and sent off your charming note, you've already succeeded.

PART I

Before

Chapter 1

Keep It to Yourself

You know the last thing in the world people want to hear from you, the very last thing they're interested in? The fact that you always have wanted to write, that you cherish dreams of being a writer, that you wrote something and got rejected once, that you believe you have it in you—if only the people around you would give you a chance—to write a very *credible*, if not great, American novel. They also don't want to hear that if you *did* start to write, there would be some things you just couldn't write about.

Your parents don't want to hear it: They want you to grow up to be a decent person, find a way to make a good living, and not disgrace the family. Your girlfriend, boyfriend, or spouse will put up with this writer-talk for weeks, months, or even years, but none of them will love you for it. Your writing, to them, is like a case of genital herpes. It's possible for them to love you, but they'll have to overlook the writing. (Have you ever seen anyone sadder or more downtrodden, more prematurely gray, than a poet's wife?) Your kids, believe me, are not going to like the idea of your writing. Think how bad it is for them when you wear gabardine slacks to a PTA meeting. Then think of the crashing humiliation they're going to suffer if you begin publishing short stories or, God forbid, a novel.

So don't tell them. Don't tell them anything about it. Especially when you're thinking about beginning. Keep it to yourself. Be discreet. Be secretive. There's time enough—all the time in the world—to let them in on the secret, to let them know who and what you really are.

Look at it from their point of view. Civilization is based on everyone "pulling together"; you may, for instance, live on a street with houses and lawns. We're expected to mow lawns, not roll around on them naked. If we own a car, we're expected to drive it, not fill it up with soft-boiled eggs. There are rules we live by, which have to do with meals three times a day and clean underwear and showing up to work on time. Absolutely everything we do is based on some structure or other: We sit on sofas and walk on treadmills and put hats on our head and shoes on our feet.

But the minute somebody begins to write—or to make any kind of real "art"—all that structure comes into question. It's no coincidence that repressive governments go after their artists and writers first. Daily life is serious business. It's hard enough to put a civilization together. And one artist is—theoretically, at least—capable of bringing down the whole damn thing.

It's my experience that you first feel the impulse to write in your chest. It's like a heartache. It's like falling in love, only more so. It feels like something criminal. It feels like the possibility of unspeakably wild sex.

So, think: When you feel the overpowering need to go out and find some unspeakably wild sex, do you rush to tell your mom about it?

In these first weeks—or months, or maybe even years—when you yearn to be a writer, especially if you live someplace that isn't L.A. or New York or San Francisco, keep your longing to yourself. If you're a guy, think of your writing as a beautiful girl and yourself as a stalker, lawless and freaky. If you're a woman, think of your writing as your lover; you certainly don't go prattling on to your husband about your lover.

The wonderful thing about your inner life is that it's your *inner* life. Think about your writing when you're making toast or suffering through a meeting at work or spacing out watching baseball on TV. Something's in your head, or your chest, that wants to get out. But keep it in there for a while.

Hemingway said—we all know this—that to talk about your work is to give it away, to weaken it, to take away its magic and its strength.

Jane Austen, they say, wrote on a sofa in the drawing room but kept a bit of sewing nearby to cover her writing in case someone came in.

Gertrude Stein got miffed when someone—was it her brother?—wasn't sufficiently appreciative of her work. "Very well, then," she said, "I will write for myself, and for strangers."

So when you're riding in the car with your husband or pushing the kids on their swings or sitting up in bed reading next to your wife and you blurt out: "I . . ." make sure you don't follow it with "... think, if I were writing a thriller, I'd set it in Martinique, because then I could use that dark skin as a symbol of philosophical negritude and the high temperatures as a symbol of hell," because you're asking for the reply—whether it's stated aloud or not—"What on God's green earth do you know about negritude, you tiresome, misguided nutcase? We already live in Barstow, where the temperature climbs well over 110 in July and August. Isn't that hell enough for you?"

Writing begins in thought. If you blurt out, "I ..." then complete the sentence with: "... always think Dijon mustard goes best on ham sandwiches, don't you?" Or "I ... vastly prefer a PC to a Mac. I'm glad that's what we bought." Or "I ... think I'll go on down to the car lot tomorrow and check out those new VW Bugs. Want to come along?"

Remember that when you start writing on a regular basis you can do it unobtrusively, on the sly. People don't have to know about it until you're confident and ready. You can be writing a thousand words a day—and one charming note or its equivalent—without anyone noticing. But you can think about writing all day and all night, the way the virtuous-seeming woman yearns for her lover or the stalker, who works behind the cash register at the convenience store, dreams about his prey.

Write your stuff, hide it, let it stack up. Reread it. Don't worry about it. Don't look for perfection. To switch metaphors, your first writing is as delicate as a seedling. Don't show it to some yahoo who wouldn't know an orchid from kudzu.

Your thousand words only takes minutes, moments. This first chapter, short but important, suggesting your first step, came in at 1,275 words and took an hour and fifteen minutes to write in the first draft. I've had years to think about silence, though, lots of time to figure out what I'm passing on to you now: Protect yourself. Be careful whom you tell. Because the last thing on earth people living an ordinary life want to hear about is how you want to be a writer.

Chapter 2

What's Your Material?

While you're being quiet, keeping your literary aspirations to yourself, pay attention to the world around you. Listen. What's your "voice," what's your material, what's your genre, what are you trying to say?

It takes a while. You can go a surprisingly long time without figuring out the kind of person you are and in what direction your life is taking you. I was thirty-two, had two kids and my Ph.D., was coming up on my second divorce, and had already written my first unpublished novel before I got the beginning of a clue. That darling second husband of mine and I had been conducting a stormy relationship for quite a while, so stormy that I found myself in therapy.

I was a frazzled hippie, and the therapist was an elegant woman with very beautiful hands, bejeweled. She whiled away her hours at work doing needlepoint. One afternoon, as I was recounting some misdeed of my short-fused husband, my voice began to rise and rise and, in the middle of a long narrative, I shouted a few times, with feeling, "I can't *stand* it! I can't *stand* it!"

Without looking up from her needlework, the therapist remarked, "Oh, you seem to be standing it all right."

It was one of those moments. I saw the little office in Beverly Hills, the two of us, one composed and amused, the other bedraggled but gaudy and caught dead to rights, busted: Queen of the long sentence. Much given to exaggeration and embellishment. *Addicted to italics.* Empress of the long-held grudge. In possession of an "Irish memory." That is to say, I could remember in photographic detail every awful thing that had ever happened to me but had a little trouble bringing back the good stuff.

But I was already beginning to publish some magazine pieces, and within the parameters of my "suffering" and my faithless husband and all that, I was beginning to have a pretty good time.

I began to listen to myself talking on the phone, because writers talk endlessly about finding their "voice," and what better way to find your voice than by *listening to your own voice*? My conversations then generally revolved around two topics: my crazy second husband—that rogue!—and my crazy nutcase mother. My vocal tone was usually a high-pitched rant-'n-rave, punctuated by rounds of hysterical laughter, because by then I knew I *seemed to be standing it all right.*

"So, you know what he did *then*? There he was, in the home of his girlfriend, and his shirt was hung right there over the doorknob—I always *wondered* what happened to that shirt—and there she is sitting on her little couch sobbing, and he's in a chair, falling over laughing, and I'm sobbing along with her and I'm saying, 'All right, Tom, you have to choose between us *right now,*' but he's laughing so hard he can't even get the words out . . ."

"So what did you do then?"

"I guess I just went home. Because I had to take care of the baby." (Voice rising again.) "Because she had that terrible *fever*! A hundred and five degrees! And he's out fucking his *brains* out with the dreaded Jennifer!"

I'm not saying I would have picked this voice, or this material. But there it was, insistent as steam from a teakettle. In my dreams, I would have had the measured, morally right voice of E. M. Forster, who wrote the best twentieth-century novels in English as far as I'm concerned, but I didn't have that voice. There was no point in trying to be "cultured." I had the education, but I didn't have the voice. At another level, I would have loved to have the voice and the material of C. S. Forester and write those terrific Horatio Hornblower novels, with a lot of eighteenth-century navy men striding the quarterdeck and having coffee and burgoo for breakfast; but it was not to be.

So, listen to your own voice. Are you a tough guy? (My second husband once called me on the phone and shouted, "What do *you* want?" then got so flustered when I reminded him that *he* made the call that he hung up.) Are you a seducer? A big silly? A philosopher—the kind of person who, whatever happens, you find yourself making up a theory about it? Are you fond of team sports? The movies? What's your small talk?

———

Now, let's go one step deeper. What's your *inner* voice talking about these days? It's always there (in my case, anyway) muttering along. Over time, if we're not mentally ill, we've learned to tune out that voice, but if you're a writer—or an artist or an actor or a comedian or a composer—it's time to tune it back in.

If you're a woman, how many times have you interrupted some guy's reverie with "What are you thinking?" (And if you're a guy, how many times have you given an automatic answer?) Imagine you're driving along in a car. Maybe you're driving or maybe you're the passenger, or—if you're a kid or a grandparent—maybe you're languishing in the back. The scenery is going by. You've driven this route a hundred times. You're in a daze. What's in there, in the daze?

Some self-help book made the statement a few years ago that men "thought about sex once every six seconds." The then-editor of the *Los Angeles Times Book Review* looked at that sentence (a few of us were hanging out in the office, choosing books to review) and blurted out, "Every six seconds! It has to be more than that!" The guys snickered; the women kept mum. But then there was more discussion, which came down to something that sounded closer to the truth: Maybe men wouldn't think about sex very much at all for hours, days, even weeks, then they'd think of it *fifty times a second*. They'd think of nothing else.

What's going on in your mind?

Here are a few things I've caught myself thinking about over the years. I think of a truck falling over a cliff and just happening to land on a convertible that has my second husband in it. That's *it*! It's all over! For weeks, days, years that thought was my constant consolation. A year ago, I gave a fairly elaborate dinner party and for as much as a month, I'm ashamed to say, my brain kept printing out: Shrimp with couscous? Couscous and shrimp? Pine nuts in the couscous? Asparagus vinaigrette or asparagus with butter and capers? Shrimp vinaigrette? Vinaigrette on the couscous? My mind pleaded with itself to stop. But that part of the mind is unregenerate. It would blare on: Five minutes to braise the shrimp? So when do you start the couscous?

Admirals and generals have loftier thoughts, but their brains probably work the same way. Flanking action? Frontal action? Flanking and frontal action? *What about a blow job?* No, that can't be right! Air strikes? Sea strikes? What about that leggy ensign?

Maybe Mother Teresa had an inner voice that was fully tuned to "aid the poor; help the dying," but most of us have stranger and more unpredictable material.

So as an artist, I might want to ask myself, why a truck coming out of the sky to obliterate poor Tom? Why not a slower, more painful death? Why is he driving a convertible when he doesn't even own one?

Mary McCarthy built a flourishing novelistic career out of shrimp-and-couscous questions, and threw in gardening questions too: "She would leave him . . . after the peonies bloomed."

———

Who are your villains; who are your heroes? (Remember, we're just thinking in a general way here, about material.) Start with your childhood—your parents, of course. Which one of them wouldn't let you go to the ball game? Which one dropped you into the deep end of the pool to see whether or not you could swim? Which one of them made fun of your clothes or made sure that you got a particularly awful haircut? Conversely, who took you fishing or typed your term papers (without grousing about it) or taught you to drive or play cribbage?

And what about those aunts and uncles? I'm telling you, this is where your treasure lies. When we're little, God deals us a hand full of kings, queens, knaves, aces. When we're young, we've got nothing much better to do than study our hand, check it out, let that material imprint itself on our memory. These people are our character actors, grown-ups who dress funny and act weird, angels who rush in unexpectedly to take our side, devils whose main mission on earth seems to be to drive us crazy, to inflict torture on us until we squeak.

Any tremors of love or lust resonating through any part of your early life? Were your parents cold to each other or were they the affectionate type? Was there a divorce in your family? My old Texan dad had a baffling saying that I didn't understand for many years: "What's bad for you is good for you; what's good for you is bad for you." A divorce feels bad while it's happening, but if you're a potential writer, that means fate has dealt you another hand: desperate women and loser men who might or might not turn into your stepparents, ready-made villains—or maybe they might play against type and turn into saviors.

What do they wear? How do they spend their time? What do their voices sound like? I was blessed by an uncle, Bob, who was so terminally devoid of social skills that he once asked me, by way of small talk, "Well, Penny, have you examined your conscience?" Another time, dead drunk but filled with rectitude, he managed to unfurl his napkin over a candle flame and set himself on fire at Thanksgiving dinner. It wasn't pleasant to sit through at the time, but as my dad said, "What's bad for you is good for you." That's the Thanksgiving I remember above all others.

Anybody *you* did wrong to? This part hurts, but it's your material. Anybody you dumped because you didn't like them anymore? Anybody you've said mean things to because you knew you could get away with it? Anybody you hauled off and slugged? Anybody whose heart you broke? How does it feel to be a heart*breaker*? How did they look and act—*exactly*—during the moments when you broke their heart? Did you feel "remorse" or a coarse joy? Or both of those things? Or something else?

Ever been in combat? In war or team sports or a long-term enmity that you didn't think would ever end?

It's a wonderful thing even to think about becoming a writer. It's like opening a crystal door in your mind. When you're trapped somewhere—in a meeting at work, or listening to a sermon in church, or while one of your parents has decided to set you straight about life, or on a date that has gone sour—when you're listening to a droning bore, you turn pain into pleasure by becoming an artist. Then it's: "Drone *on*, you hateful bore! I *love* this material!"

Wake up! Keep waking up! Wake up more and more often. Look at your life with the "keen, trained eyes of the novelist." Even if you end up writing about fifteenth-century France, the people you know now will be your characters. Your material can't belong to anyone else, only to you. Before you write even a line, you're bursting with riches.

—

When you're looking at your life, what does it look like to you? Remember the mouse in *Alice in Wonderland* who said piteously, "Mine is a long and sad tale"? Or haven't you known people who see life as one long romantic conquest? (Casanova's memoirs run to six very long volumes.) Or people who are cursed or blessed to see the sexual double meaning in every event? (My own sweet dad wrote seventy-three por-nographic novels—including a CIA tale, *Marina Blows Her Cover*—starting when he was sixty-nine, and only death stopped his output.) Is your life, so far, a tale of defeat or vic-tory or love triumphant?

What's your genre? Comic books? Soap operas? "Serious" novels? Mysteries? Romances? Westerns? Thrillers? Medical stories? Legal tales? When you think of life—*your* life—where's the action? Do you like to sue people? Or are you always get-ting sued? Do you get in bar fights? Does hurling the javelin mean the world to you? Is your life one long diet? Are you a criminal? What's your tone? Does your life strike you as funny, or is there nothing funny about it? Are you consumed by un-happiness, or do you feel lucky right now? Are you blessed by fate or are you one of life's unfortunates?

Just for fun, while you're still keeping a prudent silence about your aspirations as a writer, cast your life into different sceneries. Look up from this book and out the nearest window: Where are you?

Where are you?

Think of Larry McMurtry and the endless West Texas grass around Archer City that went into *Lonesome Dove.*

Or F. Scott Fitzgerald's hopeless infatuation with the Eastern establishment and his sense of being a Midwestern outsider that made *The Great Gatsby.*

Or Annie Proulx's deranged Newfoundland, her ferocious Wyoming; her beautiful, savage diction.

Where are you? *Where are you?* The view from your window is the view from your brain. Your voice is already there, you've been using it since you first said *Mama* and *no!* Your life is teaming with beauties and beasts, Uncle Bobs, Aunt Helens, Croats and Serbs, the men and women you detest or can't do without. "I refuse to live a life from out of the funny papers!" my father railed when he left my mom. (I believe he was rejecting a Blondie-and-Dagwood existence.) But he was more than happy, years later, to live in a structured, seventy-three-volume world of witty porn. There's no judgment in any of this. Grand opera isn't necessarily better than soap opera. All art is music to the soul.

Your voice, your characters, your worldview, your genre of choice. When you've thought about this, discreetly, for weeks or days or years, you can start—silently!—to write.

I once had a dear friend named Marc. He was young and handsome and he wanted to be a writer. He would devote his whole life and all his time to it; but to do so, he required no distractions. That meant he couldn't start to write until he stopped working. He was saving money toward that blessed, peaceful time. He was a Vietnam veteran; now he worked as a night manager in one of Los Angeles's glamorous beachside hotels.

He knew that he required silence. Yet he knew he needed to work at home. He lived with a beautiful girl in an apartment on the right side of town, but the apartment fronted on an alley. Every three or four hours a truck would drive by. Marc knew that once the truck interrupted his reverie, it might be hours, even days, before he could get back to where he had been. Just thinking about this put him in a state of despair.

What was Marc planning to write about? He wanted to write a serious historical novel about seventeenth-century Amsterdam.

Here was a man who had grown up in timber mills, who had fought and been grievously injured in an unjust war, who came home every morning from that luxury hotel with crazy tales about drugged-out beautiful people.

Marc was crammed full of stories, but "writing" meant something foreign to him. He made it into a forbidden place. He couldn't get into it: He could maybe see the seventeenth century through a very small door. What he could barely make out might have had canals and falling snow and firelight glancing off crystal chandeliers and men in velvet knee breeches, and that velvet would be dusky blue. But they would be speaking Dutch, a language he couldn't understand. Even if he'd been able to get through that door, he wouldn't have known a damn thing about what was going on. Not that he couldn't have found out, but it would have taken him years.

—

Sneak up on your material. Don't go crashing after it through the forest with a machete. Sit down, be quiet, let the material catch up with you.

Here are some more of the things that rattle around in my own mind:

• My dad left when I was eleven. My mom and I were staying at a little beach bungalow on the Balboa peninsula and he came down on Memorial Day weekend, went inside, talked to my mother while I sat on the porch steps, and then left. He walked right over me! It turned out he was a wonderfully kind divorce-dad, but he walked right over me! Three weeks later, we dropped the atomic bomb and put the entire planet in jeopardy, but he walked right over me! He was always a lot of fun and never said a word against my mother, but he . . . walked right over me.

• I need to be near a beach. I hate to get sunburned and I hate walking across the sand and I despise families who trundle junk across the beach. But I need to be near a beach! And I like hamburgers and Ferris wheels, which remind me of the beach. More than half my novels end down by a beach.

• For a while, when I was in my thirties, I had a crush on a divorced guy who lived down the hill from us in Topanga Canyon. For two years of my life, I thought: Can I see Mr. Lopez? If I go out on my balcony, I might be able to see Mr. Lopez. Is that Mr. Lopez down there? If I fix a leg of lamb, I bet I can ask Mr. Lopez for dinner. I wonder if he'll call? He could call. No, it's too late for him to call. But if I leave the house, he'll call. God knows what I ever thought I was going to do with him. But I put him (or, rather, my weird mind games about him) into my first novel. How could I have done anything else? He was stuck in my brain like a tenant who won't pay the rent and won't get out. I *still* don't know what he means, but he's part of my material.

Along with the atom bomb.

And the beach.

And my dad.

On the other hand, lumber yards, baseball, diesel engines, folk dancing aren't part of my material.

The downside to sticking with your own material is the temptation to play it safe. Years ago, when I used to teach Freshman Comp, I'd ask my students to write a short paragraph to identify themselves. They'd all give their height, sometimes their weight and their year in school and would mention that they all loved backpacking and walking on the beach. Not one of them said he had a fondness for dead moles or a predilection for eating butter by the quarter-pound. None of them were pretentious enough to say that they prayed for world peace or incautious enough to say that they yearned for their father's new trophy wife.

Backpacking and walking on the beach: What's not to like? What could be bad? But what was it that they really did? What was *really* on their minds?

For a while, again when I was in my thirties, I was "a woman alone with two children." I worked as a freelance writer for magazines—which can be about as stressful as deep-sea diving (although that's not my material, so I really wouldn't know). I taught at a small Catholic college, where the faculty was as sweet as pie but didn't understand the value of money, since most of them lived in the cushy monastery on campus. The school's policy—since the administration *did* know the value of money—was to sell half again as many parking places as there were places to park. That meant that there were never any parking places if you came after 10 A.M. Every day, I'd park illegally, and every day I'd get a twenty-dollar ticket, which I'd never pay, partly because I couldn't afford it—I took home $276 every two weeks—and partly because I resented the injustice of it all. Wasn't I a woman alone with two children? Wasn't I reduced to dating a bunch of guys who looked like the very strange fish you find at the bottom of the sea? And now the *parking authority* had embarked on a fiendish plan to extort all the pitiful monies I earned so that my children and I would starve to death!

For another two years, my entire inner life focused on the man behind the parking desk. He wore a uniform; he had a drooping mustache, like my ex-husband. He wrote me threatening letters. I flashily snubbed him when we met on this very small campus. I wanted him dead—maimed from stepping into one of the rabbit holes on the campus lawn.

No one asked me then: What do you think about when you drive the freeways, wake up in the morning, go to bed at night? What pictures flash before your eyes? And even if they had asked, would I have had the guts to admit: "I'm scared to death about what's going to happen to my kids; I'd like to squash my second husband while he's in a convertible; I'd like to run away from home and all my responsibilities, preferably to Morelia, in central Mexico, where they'll never find me and I don't even speak the language; but most of all I'd like to take that parking guy and skin him alive, one inch at a time . . ."

I took my life very seriously then, but it seems to me that this last paragraph looks like the material for an essentially comic novel, or even a novel filled with affection.

You don't have to make your material respectable. Just take a look at what's there. Let it sneak up on you.

—

Sometimes when I talk to students about this, they groan. Their lives are so boring! And just to prove it, like balky little kids, they write me a handful of papers that begin:

" 'Bbrinng!' went the alarm clock. I turned it off but it rang again. Then I got up and took a shower. Then I put on a T-shirt and sweats. Then I went downstairs from the fifth floor of Sloan Hall. Then I got some oatmeal. Then I went back upstairs and brushed my teeth."

We're all living a first draft of our lives. But when we come home from a soccer game in which we scored a goal, we don't say to our folks, "First I dropped my peanut butter sandwich. Then I got bored during math class. I forget what happened in history." No. You run home, burst into the kitchen, and say, "I scored a goal!" Notice the stuff that interests you!

—

Once you find your material, it won't let up so easily. It will blare in your ear. You'll be thinking about it all the time.

Chapter 3

A Thousand Words a Day

As soon as I realized that today I'd be writing a thousand words about writing a thousand words a day, it made me laugh. First I laughed, then I rearranged the stacks of paper on the table out on the balcony where I was writing. Then I lined up my colored pencils, and the next thing I knew, I was out in the kitchen, looking for Triscuits and tabasco, hoping I'd find a beer in the refrigerator—although it wasn't even eleven in the morning—and then I wondered if it was time to get the mail yet, and fought off the temptation to phone a girlfriend, and daydreamed mightily about the movie we're going to see this afternoon, when I get my words finished. Then I realized I desperately needed a Chapstick—not that flavorless Chapstick but the Burt's Bees kind, the kind with mentholated bees' wax. And I noticed that on my left hand my manicure was ruined.

Anything to keep from writing, as they say. That's why so many male writers commit adultery and female writers have clean houses. Because I *did* notice, when I was looking for that Chapstick, that the bookcases in the living room need dusting. And there's a long list of groceries to buy, out near the kitchen sink. And my grandson needs a birthday present; I could do that too. And I had a great lunch yesterday with a guy I went to high school with, so wouldn't it be good just to drop him a note to say thank you? Because we did have a great time. He's very personable, and strange to say, he never got married. In his whole life. Can you imagine? He did say he had a very important romance, though, for about ten years. So shouldn't I write him a thank-you note?

And after the movie, should we go to Bravo Cucina, where you can get a great pizza with a mountain of arugula in the middle, or the Crocodile, where they make those great margaritas? And I told myself I'd walk an hour a day; it's summer now and if I wait to walk until after these thousand words, it's going to be too hot.

I'm hungry.

I'm waiting for the mail.

I'm yearning for a salty margarita.

Anything to keep from writing!

——

I read somewhere that it was a good idea to write a thousand words a day. Virginia Woolf said it, and Kay Boyle. In *The Sun Also Rises,* Jake Barnes always works very hard for about two hours at a time before he goes out to nightclubs or to the track. A thousand words a day. It wouldn't work if you're a poet, but I have no idea what it's like to be a poet.

Ah, but Hemingway always said to quit while you're ahead, not to write yourself completely out of ideas on Tuesday so that you don't know where to start on Wednesday.

A thousand words a day. Another way to think of that is four pages. Four pages a day. And if you're up against it, what god in what literary heaven would punish you if you spent some of those four pages in terse, minimalist dialogue?

"Hi."

"Hi."

"Got any plans for today?"

"Fuck if I know."

"Don't use that word. You know I hate it."

"Oh, go suck some lettuce!"

"Lettuce? We don't have any lettuce. I've asked you a thousand times to go out and buy lettuce . . ."

Eight lines. If you figure twenty-six lines to a page and that nine threes make twenty-seven, I've already written a third of a page, and anybody can go ahead and write that last three and two-thirds of a page. So that's not so bad.

———

What are you going to write about? Oh my God, what are you going to *write*? I'd say, don't worry about it too much; just try to put it in fictional, literary(?!) terms. In other words, it may make you feel marginally, momentarily better to write: "My world is shit, it's totally shit, I can't go on anymore, I can't, I can't, I can't," or, "Esther's got those great boobs, they're as big as balloons, she's got two of them, great boobs, I'd like to get closer to those boobs of hers," or, "My mother hates me, *why* does she hate me, why, why, why, WHY! She never loved me. Not even when I was in my crib and she took my lunch money and gave it to my little brother, not once, not twice, but *all the time!*"

Ranting is fine. But it doesn't get you anywhere. It can be useful to read over, but it doesn't count as your thousand words unless, I suppose, you're Philip Roth, whose authentic artistic form is the rant-'n-rave.

On the other hand, when you're just starting out—and every writer in the world starts out fresh, once a day—I think it's probably okay to write, just once: "Oh my God, oh my God, what in the *world* am I going to write?" But then the only thing to do is start.

I'll write about Enrico, how he was out there in Needles, in the middle of nowhere, on a tractor—not quite a tractor, but some machine that took scoops out of the earth—and he fell into a ditch and the machine fell on top of him and, for the next couple of hours, kept taking fresh scoops out of the flesh on his back, but the most terrible thing was that for the rest of his life, when he hung out at that place in Needles—what was it called?—the whole rest of his family, about thirty of them, steered clear of the guy, and you'd see him out in the desert, where the soil was already so wrecked by alkali that they couldn't grow anything anymore. Now you'd only see him at night. (He must have lived somewhere on the property, but not at the main house.) He'd come out under the sodium lights by the gas station and limp on over to the old-fashioned soft drink machine, where the bottles stayed cold in icy water—and out in Needles it would stay up around ninety degrees at night—

and he'd get a Coke and a couple of his cousins would see him. They'd say:

"Yo, Rico."

He'd nod his head without really turning toward them.

"Howzzit goin', Ric?"

He'd ignore that. His right arm was the weak one, folded up against his chest. He'd yank the machine lid up with his left. You could almost hear the chilled rubber seal breaking, but not really. Not really, because of the zapping machines that killed a million bugs a second, but there were always a million more out here in the hot night under the lights.

It took two tries for Enrico to get the cap off the Coke. His cousins wanted not to watch him, but they did . . .

———

Well, I'm through for today. Four and a half pages, actually. If I wanted to go on with this story, I could play around with the extended family of aunts and cousins in the big house out in Needles. I'd put in a young wife who plans some infidelity, to torture not her husband but her tyrannical dad. I'd line her up some way with the tormented loner who limps around the margins of this property. I'd think of Needles, so close to the Mexican border. And wonder why people would live in such a place. And I know that one night the wife and Enrico might have an awkward late-night conversation. In the kitchen, probably.

"Oh! You scared me!"

"I, uh, needed some lettuce. I was making a sandwich and didn't have any lettuce."

She turned away as he limped heavily across faded linoleum over to the icebox.

"I don't think you'll find any. I asked Bobby to get some when he drove in to town this morning. I guess he forgot."

———

The town?

The gas station? The place in the middle of nowhere just a few miles from the Mexican border?

The kitchen?

The whitish ridges of dry dirt caked with salt that used to be fields?

A crop duster, even though there are hardly any more crops out there? But a short story is twelve pages—isn't it, more or less? How about dumping the town, doing a thousand words on the gas station, a thousand words on the people in the kitchen, and—I don't know—dividing that "dirt" stuff into two sections, one where Enrico gets his back scooped out and end with the crop duster? Or maybe the other way around?

I know I don't have to worry about it anymore, today. I've done five and a half pages! I ended up with a cup of tea and a butterscotch candy instead of that cold beer that tempted me so. I'm a writer today, and I can go to the movies with a clear conscience. I've done *more* than a thousand words!

And I certainly don't have to write that man from high school a thank-you note, and the dust in the living room can wait another day. I'm in a state of grace now, until tomorrow morning. I've written my thousand words. And had some fun doing it.

—

How come I suggest *a thousand words a day five days a week for the rest of your life?* Why not five thousand words a day one day a week, or—as some poor, disgruntled student of mine once heard it—a thousand pages a day seven days a week for the rest of your life?

It's a thousand words a day because anyone can do four pages. It's five days a week for two reasons: 1) Five days a week makes it sound to you and the outside world like you're "working," and anything you can do to placate the snapping dogs in the outside world is good for you and writers everywhere; 2) momentum. It takes a pretty strong effort of will to start any project; it only takes about half as much energy to keep a project going. (And, as Hemingway pointed out, if you keep a little something left over from the day before, it's fairly easy to get started, and if you get started the next day, it won't be long until you finish.)

The whole world will sometimes conspire to keep you from doing that, though. For instance: Yesterday, I was up and out on the balcony bright and early; the phone didn't ring, I got inspired by that remembered landscape of Needles, I realized later that "lettuce" came into it because new butter lettuce is at the market right now, and it tastes great with shallots and balsamic vinegar, and I'd had some braised iceberg lettuce at a Chinese restaurant earlier this week. So, *lettuce!* How ingenious! Isn't it amazing how your life gets incorporated into your inner life, and so on. I did my thousand words.

But today it's two-thirty in the afternoon before I get out on the balcony. Last night I picked up some boxes of stuff that belonged to my dead mother. This morning my daughter Clara came over and we started going through it—old photos, report cards starting from my mom's second and third grades and up through high school. Clara's girlfriend came back from Nepal, so we both talked on the phone to her. Clara made some more phone calls and used the fax machine while I read another newspaper and fiddled around putting some of Mother's family pictures in with our own. By the time Clara left, it was noon, and I hadn't even had breakfast.

And Clara came by so early that I didn't even get a shower.

Which might explain why, despite a nice—actually a great—morning, I began to think that my life is passing and I'm *wasting* it. I'm literally *wasting my time!* And in the same way that once you go off your diet with one sugar doughnut you might as well eat the whole damn box, a kind of sluggish sweat dampens my skin: It's only an hour until *Oprah* comes on, and I can do some shopping after that and cook something really simple for dinner.

Besides, *who is ever going to know* whether I write that forever-cursed one thousand words or not? Isn't there a phrase that covers this situation: "Let's not and say we did"? I wrote almost six pages yesterday. Can't I just write six pages tomorrow, and won't that average out to that slimy, hateful thousand words a day? Who the hell even *cares*? It's not as though the publishing world in New York, three thousand miles away, is waiting with bated breath.

The day is spoiled, irrevocably spoiled; even if I *do* write my thousand words, it's going to be four in the afternoon before

I'm done: What am I doing even calling myself a writer? I can't even get up off this *couch*!

The truth is the only one who will know (or care) about those thousand words is you. If you only write two pages—or no pages—on a Tuesday, don't try to make it up on Wednesday: Each day is a new day, with its four blank pages waiting. You can never "catch up." You can't raise or lower the numbers to play in your favor. (A rough analogy to this comes from the years when I taught at that small Catholic college mentioned earlier: We had plenty of time and very little money, and we'd eat brown-bag lunches and tell stories from our own Catholic childhoods. One darling man remembered that he went through months of hell: Kids are supposed to go to confession every Saturday afternoon so that their souls will be bright and shining on Sunday morning, but this boy—I'll call him Ralph—sinned a lot against the Sixth and Ninth Commandments—those cover impure thoughts—say, ten times in one week. He'd be terrified to go to confession. That's doing it more than once a day! So he'd skip Saturday confession and pretend to have a cold on Sunday (thus missing mass, and committing another mortal sin). He'd sin against the Sixth and Ninth Commandments *twenty-four* times in the second week! Ten added to twenty-four is thirty-four times in fourteen days. Four weeks and a sin count in the high triple digits later, plus all the other sins, up to and including lying to his mother about being sick, Ralph would finally go to confession, where the priest sighed deeply, gave him a good talking-to, and handed out a very stiff penance.

Then, if he could only make it as a "pure" person from Saturday night until Sunday after mass, Ralph would have at least the ghost of a chance of making it to heaven if he died in his sleep. And *then,* if he could only keep the numbers down . . .

But of course it wasn't going to happen.

It's only four pages, five days a week. It won't kill you. You can't "fall behind" and you can't "get ahead." Every day is a new one thousand words.

Saturday is for errands, Sunday for rest, picnics, spiritual renewal. That's the way it's supposed to be. For the rest of your life. Or until you get tired of it. But wouldn't it be wonderful if you didn't get tired of it?

—

I want to stress again that your thousand words are best when they're *not* just outpourings of raw feeling. Sometimes those raw feelings point to real emotion, though—primitive arrows that suggest what you really might want to be writing about. I remember a friend who had the Great Novelist Syndrome pretty bad. He drank heavily, was prone to bringing out his bullfighter's cape around midnight and practicing media-veronicas in the street with nonexistent bulls. He groaned so much about his lost talent and abandoned dreams that his young wife called his bluff: They'd move to the idyllic island of Catalina for two years; she'd work to support the family. All he'd have to do was take care of the kids and write the Great American Novel.

Poor guy. Before he knew it, he was stuck in some long, end-less narration about a man who lived the bohemian life in Paris, subsisting on lentils and making love to sulky women. Every afternoon his wife would come home, give him a cool appraising stare, and then make dinner. Eventually, he gave the manuscript to my husband and me to read, and it was ghastly, except for a riveting passage somewhere in the middle of chapter 32, where the double spaces changed to single-space and went something like this:

Goddamn, goddamn, goddamn, if those kids don't stop screaming I'm going to KILL them! No, I'll kill myself and then I'll kill them. Why did I ever marry that bitch-cow; she's trapped me, I'm dying, I'm drowning, I can't hear myself THINK, she knew what would happen, she set me up, I'll kill her, then I'll kill myself but not before I kill those FUCKING KIDS.

Tyrone eased himself into the crowded café and lit up a Gauloise. He wondered if Madeleine would be in the café today. He was running short of francs. He was down to his last sou (centime?). If Madeleine didn't come in to the café soon, he would have to order lentils again . . .

If our friend had read his own manuscript carefully, he might have decided to scrap lentil-boy and write instead about a handsome surfer type with far-fetched artistic dreams who's tricked by his sensible yet guileful wife into facing up to his own failures—all this against the background of an "island paradise" that turns out to be hell.

Catalina at the time was as beautiful as Portofino, with flying fish and neighborhood baseball teams and celebrities sailing in every weekend and a local population who drank way too much. It was all there—literally under his nose. His own story. It obsessed him, drove him nuts, but he could only put it down in incoherent bursts of raw emotion. He couldn't find his way to it.

What if you look for the raw emotion in your own world and then, instead of dissipating it in single-spaced howling, just for the hell of it, write your own story? Not the Great American Novel, for God's sake, just a story that interests you. Suppose you keep a Post-it nearby that says: *Character? Plot? Geography? Point of view? Time and space? Building a scene? Rewriting? Dialogue vs. description?*

And without looking at that list until later (maybe five days later, or six months later) you dash off a thousand words, remembering, in a vague sort of way, that what you're writing should have characters, that they have to do something, that you'll have to think about point of view and where the story's happening, and that it's wonderful if your characters actually say things. At some point, you'll have to decide on the beginning, the middle, the end; but not now.

It's supposed to be fun. Suppose you decide where it would be a treat to write—out in a park, where they can't find you? In the back booth of a coffee shop? At the beach? By a lake? In a bar? At the track? At your office during lunch, or early in the morning before anyone comes in? I prefer the couch in my living room, generally speaking, or the balcony in the new place I'm living. Or the dining room table for a change of pace. I like to have some coffee or tea or, when I'm doing heavy revision, some red wine to cool down my anxiety. Or a glass filled with blueberries and white wine.

I like to play music: Gerry Mulligan and Chet Baker or, more often, Van Morrison. His whispered words buoy me up:

"Listen to the lion."

"Meet me down by the pylons."

"No guru, no message, no preacher."

Classical music is wonderful, *if you love it*. This part is all for you. You can construct a little hut for your soul with everything it needs ready at hand. Remember, it's no big deal, but it's a *huge* deal. You're only having "fun," but if you're lucky, your soul, your *real* soul, will come out and say hi, say a few words.

A thousand words a day. Five days a week. For the rest of your life.

Chapter 4

Charming Notes

My old Texan dad knew himself to be an extraordinary cook. He loved to whomp up dishes that would make "Saint Simon Stylites shimmy on down off his pillar." He was particularly proud of his chili. He devised a labor-intensive, very elaborate 18-hour chili that involved hand-chopping chuck, sautéing—then marinating—salt pork, doing the beans from scratch, of course, throwing in ground cocoa and fresh brewed coffee. At the end, you had the greatest chili in the world, bar none. You could take the lid off the pot and wait for Saint Simon.

Or in a pinch he could fry up some ground beef, garlic, and chili powder, a can of beans, and a can of tomatoes. That was his 18-minute chili, and it was pretty good too.

As I said in the introduction, I guess this book is the 18-hour version of how to make a literary life. The 18-minute version, simplicity itself, is in this paragraph: a thousand words a day (or two hours of revision) five days a week, for the rest of your life, and—*and!*—one charming note (or a phone call that makes your hands sweat), five days a week, for the rest of your life.

My students *hate* to hear about writing those charming notes. They look as blank and uncomprehending as a bed of broccoli when I suggest to them—again!—that all writing, all art, maybe all of *life,* is exactly like dating. Life is a matter of courtship and wooing, flirting and chatting. If you don't know a soul in the literary world, you can choose to stay home and sulk until the cows come home. You can write stuff and look at it and agonize and worry and wait five years and send something out to a periodical where they've never heard of you and a bored clerk or intern will send it right back with a printed rejection slip. And that could be either because you're a misunderstood genius or because everything you write is awful. Or because you're disorganized or you don't proofread.

Or it could be that they don't know you from Adam, and, like everyone else in the world, they like to hang out with their friends instead of with strangers.

If you're born and raised in an upper-middle-class (or higher) family in New York or New England, you might never have to write a note to a stranger. Your grandfather might have attended college with Norman Mailer; your grandmother might have gone to that Episcopal church where Madeleine L'Engle goes. You probably summer in the Hamptons.

But some of us have to make our own literary lives.

Back in the thirties and early forties, a young American woman named Kay Boyle wanted to live a literary life. Like many people, she knew what she wanted, but she didn't know how to get it. She married a Frenchman, on the grounds that living anywhere in France is practically like living in Paris (and everyone knew that the literary and artistic life had been *cracking* there in the twenties). But it didn't work out the way she'd planned.

Kay Boyle found herself in some dim, damp town in coastal France. Her husband was a tire salesman—a *tire* salesman! The first place they lived didn't even have windows.

So Boyle bought some paint and painted some windows on her windowless walls with bright, great views. Then she started writing letters to everyone in Paris she'd ever wanted to know. She admired their work, and told them a little about her own; she sent stories to periodicals and letters to men and women who were living the life she so passionately craved. Her plan worked out. She literally wrote herself *out* of that windowless cave, left the Frenchman, went into the life she'd always wanted, in which she published wonderful stories and wore a velvet cloak and fell madly in love and danced, and stayed out late and produced beautiful novels and partied so hard that she finally came down with spinal meningitis.

That—and World War II—told her it was time to settle down, so she eventually married a wonderful man, came home to America, had a flock of kids, taught writing at a respected university, wrote, and wrote some more, and in her late sixties was sighted by a reliable witness making out passionately with a man one-third her age at a writers' conference. She lived many more years after that and was loved and respected by all.

Of course, she could have elected to do nothing and ended up the snippy, resentful wife of a tire salesman in a house without windows.

—

For years, when *I* was a young wife, I'd go about my house-work dreaming of E. M. Forster. If only I could tell him what *The Longest Journey* had meant to me! (And even now, sitting on this balcony, I think about how *A Room with a View* changed my life, so that since I was thirty, I've always lived in places with beautiful vistas and prospects and views. If I hadn't read that particular novel, I might have spent my adulthood peering into some backyard or other, with a fence, and maybe an alley behind it. Nothing against backyards, but Forster literally and figuratively *changed my life*. And I wanted so much to tell him that.

Then he died. But guess what? There had been months, even years, when I could have written him a note to say thank you. Thank you for reminding me I'm not totally alone on this earth; thank you for teaching me about morality and passion in a way I can respect; thanks for teaching me that profound and simple thing about views: that everyone and everything looks better against a background of violets that "spot the grass with azure foam."

Maybe he would have written me back. Maybe, in Cambridge, even with all his distinguished friends, he would have liked to have thought of a housewife in California reading his books with so much love and respect and trying to get what he was trying to say.

—

So I strongly suggest that in addition to your thousand words a day, you write one charming note to a novelist, an editor, a

The Four - Fold Way

author Arien

HOTEL BEACON

2130 BROADWAY AT 75TH STREET
NEW YORK, N.Y. 10023
TEL. (212) 787-1100 FAX (212) 724-0839

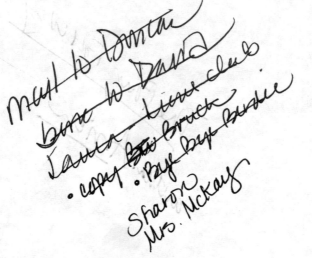

journalist, a poet, a sculptor, even an agent whose professional work or reputation you admire, *five days a week, for the rest of your life.* Then after you write the note, you address it, put a stamp on it, and mail it out. These notes are like paper airplanes sailing around the world, and they accomplish a number of things at once.

They salute the writer (or editor or agent) in question. They say to him or her: Your work is good and admirable! You're not laboring in a vacuum. There are people out in the world who know what you do and respect it.

The notes are also saying: I exist, too. In the same world as you. Isn't that *amazing*? They can also say: Want to play?

These notes are just *notes.* You don't want to burden some poor wretch with the entire story of your life. You absolutely don't want to ask them for a favor, as in: "Hello. I really like your work. Enclosed please find my 800-page manuscript on giant lizards who live under the earth—and throw massive lizard conventions!—in the state of Arizona." Don't offer to go and live with them. Remember what your mother taught you about thank-you notes (if she bothered). Be gracious. You're entering into an emotional and spiritual courtship with the literary world that will last the rest of your life.

—

From my point of view, charming notes are best written on "half-sheets," stationery that is five by eight inches. (If you're broke, or excessively pure of heart, you can take a standard eight-and-a-half-by-eleven-inch piece of white typing paper and fold it in half.) The paper can be as cheap or expensive as you like. Whatever you decide, it's going to say a lot about you. There should be some kind of identification at the top. Joan Didion has stiff, pale blue cards with JOAN DIDION embossed in silver. Herbert Gold prefers a larger sheet of white paper with his name and address "carelessly" jammed down any old way with a blurry rubber stamp. Tommy Thompson, God rest his soul, favored beige cards with his name printed in dark brown. Now that there are Kinko's everywhere, you can order up something with a minimum of fuss.

Your stationery should not have flowers on it. It should not be in the form of a greeting card with a Manet or Monet reproduction on the front. The stationery should be about *you*, not some French Impressionist. It shouldn't be unnervingly clever, unless *you're* unnervingly clever. It should be as classy as you can stand it to be.

Postcards are an interesting alternative to this, although in no way do they replace your charming-note stationery. But every once in a while you'll find the perfect postcard, and it's worth stocking up on them: They show your state of mind, and when you're too absolutely depressed to write a real charming note, you can dash off a couple of cards. My two favorite cards over the years have been a pattern of tropical flowers from a pretentious restaurant here in Santa Monica, called Ivy at the Shore, and a devastatingly desolate picture of the first highway across the Mojave Desert (sold in the little town of Victorville, where my mother used to live), hauntingly called the Old Plank Road. That's what it was—two or three planks stuck out in a bunch of sand. Sometimes I feel cool enough to send "Ivy at the Shore"; sometimes "The Old Plank Road" is the best I can do.

Personally, I've always hated to type and I'm rather proud of my handwriting, so I hand-write my notes with a black Flair pen. Many male writers—probably just for their charming notes—keep an old manual typewriter around the house. I have an interesting collection of typewritten postcards from John Updike, explaining why he would never, under any circumstances, come to California. His typewriter was actually capable of something *less* than single-space, and of course the cards were scrunched in the typewriter any old way, so the lines ran into and jammed up against each other. He had so *much* to say, the "graphic" message indicated, that he didn't even have time to type straight. The text ran into the return address, and the picture on the other side was some melancholy, tasteful East Coast landscape. A world away from the Old Plank Road! But that's what happens with these charming notes. Worlds get in touch with each other.

Sometimes these notes will be so exquisite that no one will ever throw them away! I still have a beautiful letter that Joan Didion wrote me when she learned I was going to Bali. She recommended a place called—was it the Tanjun Sari?—"a small but esteemed compound," and such was my awe of Joan Didion, and my total, literal-minded belief in her prose style, that I immediately conjured up a *compound:* a patch of bare red earth stamped almost to glass by generations of bare feet, dotted by a series of small separate buildings with thatched roofs, lit by oil lamps, or torches, maybe, and strewn with bevies of bare-breasted maidens. But they would all be very mannerly, because this was an *esteemed* compound.

The prices were too steep for us, it turned out, but we spent a couple of afternoons at the Tanjun Sari. It had mini-refrigerators in every room, a swimming pool with a bar in the middle of it, where you sat on a stool up to your neck in water and sipped tropical drinks. The only bare-breasted beauties were a flock of cruelly sunburned American starlets, who were being yelled at in Polish by Roman Polanski. "A small but esteemed compound"! On that perfect blue paper with her silver name on top. "A small but esteemed compound" still lives as a phrase in our family's vocabulary, and that note is tucked away in Special Collections at UCLA forever. Just too gorgeous to ever throw away.

A couple of weeks ago I struck up a conversation with a distinguished man at a literary party. (How I love those things! It's immature, I know, and I should be above all that at my age, but a glass of white wine, some hors d'oeuvres, and a conversation with someone who's just had a book come out makes me so happy!) I'd never read his work, and he'd never read mine, but we stood out on a pretty little terrace and exchanged addresses and promised to send each other our books. But in addition to the book he'd written, he sent me a book of blank pages with wooden covers that he'd bound himself. Luckily, in addition to my novels, I had a copy of a coffee table book of antique postcards my family and I had put out under the name of Monica Highland, and I batted that back to him in the mail. A week later, he sent me one of the coolest charming notes I've ever seen, a landscape watercolor running thirty-six-by-four inches, with the last four inches taken up by the charming note—written in Flair pen, filled with compliments, sprinkled with Spanish words like *pues* and *bueno,* and there, stretched out to the left, this long and lovely California watercolor. (Which came first, the note or the painting? How did he achieve such effortless perfection?) I framed it, because it was *too wonderful to ever throw away.*

———

Again, my students hate the whole idea of charming notes. "What are we supposed to *say?*"

I answer, "Why not divide the note into three paragraphs of three lines each—the first one about their work that you like so much, the second saying who you are and why the work touched you, the third suggesting politely that you're looking forward to the next thing they're going to write."

And this is when my students go through agony. They turn gray when they finally realize I'm not kidding, that they really *are* going to have to send a couple of charming notes in order to get out of the class. What happens next is like a really theatrical, flamboyant consciousness-raising seminar. You get to see people slamming into their own personally erected emotional brick walls, their "hokeyness barriers," if you will.

Students say: "I'm not going to kiss up to anybody!" Or, "What! Do you want me to be a *brownnose?*" Or, "Won't these notes just make them mad?" Or, "I'm not going to *sell out!*" Or, "I know *you* think writing is nothing but a *business,* but *I . . .*"

But then there comes a time, usually a couple of weeks before the end of the quarter, when they bleakly realize that they're not going to be saved by a 10-point earthquake that will destroy all of Los Angeles and relieve them from the obligation of writing those goddamn charming notes.

Some students resort to one last desperate measure. They write to a couple of dead people, hoping against hope I won't notice that Wilkie Collins or Agatha Christie has already left the planet. Others gnash their teeth and send out these little missives. Then sometimes they sail in to class with wide, astonished smiles. "Jane Smiley wrote me back! She says she's glad I liked *A Thousand Acres*!" Or, "Anne Lamott says she's tickled to death I read *Rosie*." Or one sweet woman came in, beside herself, with a nice note from Michael Crichton.

It's a little like getting a note from Snow White or the angel Gabriel. There's a wonderful feeling to it.

Of course, you may not get an answer. Somebody somewhere may be holding your innocent little note between two nicotine-stained fingers, snickering, in his haughtiest voice, "Can you believe it? Some rube from Waverley, Ohio, says he likes my work! Well, *that* certainly makes my day!"

So what? So what, so what, so what.

—

"There's no one on this earth I'd even think of writing to!" said one of my students, a young woman, scowling.

"Oh, there must be somebody whose work you like!"

"No. There isn't *anyone,* and besides, nobody knows where she lives."

"Couldn't you write her in care of her publisher?"

"No!"

"Couldn't you look her up in *Contemporary American Authors*? Because at the end of those articles, they usually have an address where you can find them. Or look her up on the Internet."

"It says she doesn't have a permanent home. She prefers to live anonymously. Nomadically. In hotels."

She gives me a wild grin. The rest of the class looks on with interest. They see it! The woman's heart, her true and only soul, is desperately involved in this. She cares so much about this writer (and all the things this writer means to her) that the thought of writing to her is as awful as jumping out of a plane without a chute.

But some people sky-dive.

"Just tell me her name."

Reluctantly, she does.

"Well, I know where she lives!"

"I'm not writing to her!"

"Okay. Do you have any money around?"

"Maybe."

"Why not send her some balloons?"

"Huh?"

"Some helium balloons. Because her work really is light, and it really does shine. You can write *I love your work* on a card, can't you? Or have the balloon guy write it?"

She does. She sends the balloons. And ends up having an intense, real, delightful romance with the literal woman of her dreams. Everybody's life was changed for the better. The hotel where that writer used to stay folds around a charming inner court with a stained-glass dome. I like to think of those helium balloons going up that court through golden air, light and delicate as all our aspirations.

Chapter 5

Pretend to Be a Writer

You've thought and thought about being a writer. You've bought yourself some stationery; you've written some notes to people you admire. You've begun writing those one thousand words a day, five days a week—*more or less*—for the rest of your life. But (maybe because you've been keeping it a secret?) your life seems, on the outside at least, a little bit boringly the same. Wasn't this supposed to be transformational, at some level? And here you are still looking and acting like everybody else.

You're pumping gas in Tulsa—or Mossman, if you're in Australia. You're making Krispy Kremes on the morning shift in San Antonio. You're a housewife in Durham, sitting in your living room after the kids have gone off to school, feeling blank. The answers to your charming notes haven't come in yet. Maybe no one will *ever* write back to you.

And just because you've been writing your thousand words a day doesn't make you a writer! Your gas-pumping buddies would laugh themselves sick. Your ex-bridesmaids would snicker.

If you can't really believe you're a writer, why not *pretend* you're one? You pretended when you were little; why not now? If you were a writer, what would you have? A black turtleneck sweater? Maybe, but that won't fly if you live in the Mojave Desert. A cigarette-smoking habit, so you can have yourself photographed in wreaths of smoke? No. You'll die, with people yelling at you for being dumb.

We're in a new century now. You get to define yourself *and* literature just the way you choose. Bob Shacochis seems, from the outside at least, to follow in the "man's" presentation of the literary man. He has a good build and suns himself by any available pool; he lives, or did live, in a van built for extensive travel. He has a beautiful wife. He owns two vigorous Irish setters, who always need to be taken for a walk. That's one way.

Or think of Amy Tan, who dresses in extraordinary "Oriental" costume, heavy on the silks and satins. She's the only person on earth I know who has not one but *two* tiny dogs rattling and barking around in her purse. I'm told that the dogs are an ingenious coping device, something to deflect the hundreds of Chinese readers who come up to her to say, "My grandmother says the way your grandmother cooked mung beans is all *wrong*!" Instead, usually held quite close to her chest, are two alive and furry creatures with bright eyes and pointy noses and an occasional *yap!* So Amy's readers are reduced to saying, "Oh, how cute!" And if they're very devoted fans, too starstruck to say anything at all, they too can manage to utter, "Oh, how cute!" So Amy Tan is a writer, and she has those glorious costumes, and a couple of useful dogs.

—

I'd been wearing black turtlenecks (in brightest Southern California, where young actors and artists or cool dudes of every kind still manage to wear black on black *in* black, to paraphrase the Marvin Gaye song) but not thinking too much about it when I found myself putting together a "first annual" writing conference at Loyola Marymount University.

Writers in general are very nice people. That's why I was surprised, talking to Harlan Ellison one morning, when he told me he'd be speaking for at least four hours, because that's how long he always spoke.

"I have you scheduled for eleven A.M.," I said. "Then there's the lunch hour, I guess you can speak through that. But everyone else is only talking for an hour, Mr. Ellison. Don't you think that's long enough?"

"I always speak for at least four hours," he said. "And I'll need you to provide a case of Perrier, chilled, and a dozen limes. Of course, I'll be bringing my own lectern. I expect soundmen at the ready to hook up my speaker system."

"We have a lectern," I said weakly. "We have one right up there on the stage."

Harlan Ellison raised his voice. He was bringing his own lectern; he expected his case of Perrier, his dozen limes. And, of course, he'd be speaking for four hours. Maybe five.

We scheduled him at 8 P.M. on the third night, after dinner and before the Saturday-night party. The auditorium was packed; he had plenty of fans. He had placed hundreds of remaindered copies of his books on tarpaulins on the damp lawn outside. We realized why he had demanded his own lectern, a diminutive little gadget made of wrought iron: He was so short that he would have had to stand on a chair to be seen if he'd used the ordinary one.

He cracked open a Perrier, squeezed in some lime, and was just beginning to settle in to a long-winded tirade when the woman who ran the conference bookstore came screeching down the aisle, accusing Ellison of restraining free trade by undercutting her prices for his books. He howled like a castrated bison; she responded with shrieks from *The Texas Chainsaw Massacre.*

What a spectacle! The pretty little lectern, the screaming science-fiction writer, the raving—but glamorous—bookseller. Evidently, Ellison had known *exactly* what he wanted, and he got it: attention, a drama, sales. He went on talking for about two and a half hours, until people began to drift over to the party. By midnight, he and the bookseller were locked dreamily in each other's arms on the dance floor. He'd sold bushels of books and obviously had a wonderful time.

So, if you were a writer, what would you want? Hemingway wanted to spend his life outside the borders of the United States, and he picked great places to live: France, Spain, Cuba. He must have wished at some point for affectionate, affluent wives, because all of his brought lots of dollars to their marriages.

Richard Ford must have wished for a madly dashing trench coat, because I saw him once, at a reception given by the American ambassador in Paris, at the center of a circle of fans, smoking, swathed in a madly dashing trench coat. (Writers don't just *appear* that way, sprung from the head of literary Zeus; there's a moment in time when they stop by the haberdashery and get fitted.) Hemingway's he-man image came initially from a single photography session—set up by his prescient editor, Maxwell Perkins—where he was decked out in a rough-looking fisherman's sweater.

We all know that Anne Rice has been known to jump into a coffin. When she's on tour with those wonderful vampire books, she prefers to be the last one on a plane and the first one off; she travels with an endless supply of Tab, and requests that the ordinary contents of each hotel minibar, from each hotel room she spends the night in, be filled with Tab and nothing else.

But remember what *you* want. You're creating a world of icons and talismans. Anything that you can do to pretend to be a writer—do it. If you feel that the only way you can begin to write is against a background of mountains, you may want to pull out the atlas and check out mountain towns. When you close your eyes and dream of what you want, do you see the ocean? There's plenty of it on both sides of America.

Do you need or want a personal assistant? Such a thing might seem presumptuous or beyond your reach. But a teenager working for you at minimum wage for eight or ten hours a week can change your life.

Every writer needs an entourage. You need an entourage so that when your book comes out and you start having signings, you won't be quaking with terror and sorrow in front of a bunch of empty folding chairs. "Writers must stick together like beggars or thieves," Hemingway said, and he was right. As a writer, you never want to go anywhere alone if you can help it. Start thinking now about your entourage, what it's going to look like and how much fun you're going to have. You can begin by saying—to your very trusted friends—"If I ever publish anything, will you be part of my entourage?"

Or maybe you'd like bodyguards. At a very flossy university reception, Maya Angelou impressed me—and everybody else—by showing up with a trio of muscular escorts. I'm not sure who or what they were protecting her from—some bespectacled assistant professor who might run amok? But she sure seemed to get a kick out of those bodyguards. Somewhere along the line, young, disrespected, and ignored, Angelou must have thought, By God, when I make it, I'm going to get myself some bodyguards!

Do you want lovers? So many people—especially men, I imagine—think wistfully: Once I get to be a writer, I'm going to have so much sex it will make me dizzy! Here in Los Angeles, many of us remember the man—back in the days of typewriters—who made a tape cassette of himself typing and swearing, locked in the throes of creation. After breakfast, if his wife was at home, he'd retire virtuously to the back bedroom to write, turn on the cassette, and spend the morning phoning up his girlfriends, arranging a daunting schedule of magic afternoons. I think it probably is true that writers (and artists, college professors, actors, and actresses) get to have more magic afternoons than the general population. It's a pleasing side effect of not having to work regular hours. It's also a corollary of leading a double or triple life. You've got the life you're living, the life you're writing about; sometimes it's hard to avoid the gluttonous temptation to layer in another life or two, just for the hell of it. And *anything to keep from writing!*

—

Years ago, making a list of goals, I decided that I wanted a) to win the Nobel Prize or be too good for it. I guess I'm too good for it, because the people from Stockholm still haven't come knocking. But what that goal did do for me was keep my intentions lofty. With very few exceptions, I've been able to write what I thought might help the world. I wanted b) to have a family life that "both glitters and is stable." This was a big one for me. My father always set his "literary life" out of the house in exotic circumstances he could never get to. I wanted a literary life inside my own walls. I wished for a family that was one big "entourage" for one another, where we could edit or collaborate or drink champagne and make one another laugh, and the main miracle in my own life is that we've been able to live that out. But it's like Richard Ford's dashing trench coat: It doesn't just happen; you have to think of it first, make arrangements for it. (I also wished for c) a safe, painless, and interesting death. We'll see how that pans out. But I hope my death will involve plenty of euphoric painkilling drugs and people stopping by to say hi.)

I don't care much for clothes, but I like adornment, and for every book I've finished I've bought myself a gift, because I think a writer—*this* writer!—should have a few pieces of serious jewelry. And when I begin a new book, I buy a set of new CDs that I'll play and play until the book is done. I believe in having a view. I've lived in the mountains, and now I live by the beach.

At a PEN awards dinner a few years ago, I re-met a wonderful Nigerian writer who'd been in prison in his own country. I'd known him earlier, in different circumstances, when he'd been a quiet guy on a Getty scholarship wearing khakis and Izod shirts. Now, back in America, out of prison, about to receive an award, he was dressed up in great dazzling lengths of pink chiffon, with another fruff of iridescent pink upon his handsome head. He was transcendentally happy, and he shone. That's what writers should look like, in their hearts and souls at least, raising the consciousness(!) of the entire civilized world.

—

Just this morning, on some television talk show, I watched as a sweet Las Vegas cocktail waitress mused about having won $35 million from a very generous slot machine. She has eight brothers and sisters and a mom and a boyfriend, and she was planning on dividing the money—half to the boyfriend, the rest to her brothers and sisters and mom. But wasn't she going to do anything for herself? Yes, she might go on a vacation with her family and catch a few shows she'd missed . . .

How we are limited by the poverty of our dreams! And writing this, I see that—for all my exhorting and preaching—I'm limited too. I notice that "what I'd want if I were a writer" includes very little in the realm of adventure. I never want to see a jungle close up (I did some of that when I was very young, and jungles, to me, are just one big mosquito). I don't want to climb Everest or any other mountain. I'd just as soon skip going to India, because I'm afraid I'd get sick. I want the travel I do to be wrapped in false glamour and ersatz romance and as much luxury as I can afford. I guess I saw enough poverty starting out that I'm not interested in it. A hotel room with no windows, lit by a single bar of fluorescent light—even if it's in Kathmandu? No. When I daydream, I see waiters in white jackets.

I don't think of committing criminal acts—although what an idea to embark on a career of larceny or fraud or bank robbery purely for the business of "research."

And just now, looking for a scrap of paper to write down some notes, I came upon an ad in a magazine for flesh-colored foam-rubber breasts. "Far better," the ad says, "than silicone implants. And only $59.99!" My dreams don't include anything with silicone or rubber.

And think of the things I haven't even thought of because I haven't even thought of them! Skis. A chalet in Switzerland. (Those must have been Irwin Shaw's dreams.) Ringside seats at boxing matches (Joyce Carol Oates's dream, since she writes so delightfully on boxing.) A snazzy yacht docked in a Mediterranean port (Harold Robbins's dream).

The most "outrageous" thing I'm ever apt to do on any given day is talk to a stranger when I'm standing in line at the supermarket. But there are other things in my life as a writer that I've longed for and gotten: a sweet circle of wonderful writing friends who love and support one another. I wanted it and I got it, and I'm so grateful. Now, when doubting students say, "Oh, I don't want to get too close to writers. They're so mean and competitive. I mean, look at Hemingway!" I can say, with perfect, grateful honesty, "No, I know a *lot* of writers, and there's not a bad one out there that I know. They're generous to a fault. And funny!"

I yearned for the perfect editor—the one who understands your prose and takes you for a spin out on the cosmic dance floor so that in all the world there's just the two of you, dancing in sentences, and he—or she—never steps on your feet, and you're graceful too, and you have fun together, and neither of you says anything mean. I've been cosmically lucky with my editors. Thank you, Harry Sions, Marshall Lumsden, Dan Weaver, Joe Kanon, Ann Godoff, Lee Boudreaux, Dwight Whitney. You're beyond my wildest dreams.

I daydream that someone will write my biography so that perhaps readers will know what it was like to be a woman writer in the Out Crowd in the twentieth and twenty-first centuries. We'll see. We'll see.

I knew, from reading incessant "lives" and anthologies and memoirs about the Bloomsbury group, that besides snapshots documenting your memories and good times, you need a portrait by a famous artist, and I've got one by Don Bachardy, who lived with Christopher Isherwood just one canyon down from us on the beautiful Pacific coast. Bachardy painted my daughters, too, and these portraits, gentle reminders that we're alive, bolster my life as a writer on days when I feel poorly: because Isherwood knew Virginia Woolf, and Bachardy knew Isherwood, and I know Bachardy. And the paintings are great!

Life has a way of kicking up treats, giving you presents you didn't even know you wanted. Five years ago, I was diagnosed with macular degeneration, a fairly disgusting eye disease that does away with your central vision, making it harder and harder, and then finally impossible, for you to read or write or drive. I took it very hard, walking around in a haze of despair and fear until I remembered: Wait! I'm a writer, trained as a journalist, a novelist, not some weeping *victim*! I took a set of trips I never would have taken, met some people I never would have known, found treatments I never knew existed. So all that was good. My ability to read stabilized, and I went back to driving in the daytime. But I still couldn't drive at night. And in L.A. that's a curse.

At last, desperate, I called up an outfit called Affordable Limo. The "Affordable" appealed to the mousy writer in me who cares nothing about clothes. The "Limo" appealed to the better, more fearless part: Damn the expense! I deserve the very best and now is the time for it!

So I met Albert, my driver. How could I not have known that "a writer like me"—the writer I've been pretending to be all these years—never ventures out at night without a town car and her own impeccable driver?

Albert has glistening, dark suits and perfect manicures. He laughs immoderately at all my jokes. At a book signing recently, as he lounged against the car, someone asked him, "Are you Carolyn's husband or what?" He answered, in his wonderful English accent, "Her *what*."

I know Albert is a jazz musician who only moonlights part-time driving cars, and I know—all too well!—that I'm a woman with a very tiresome case of macular degeneration; but I'm not all that interested in reality, not in this chapter. I'm *pretending to be a writer!* I know that a thousand words a day and one charming note and a lot of heartfelt pretending makes strong magic.

Chapter 6

Hang Out with People
Who Support Your Work

Influenced by my dad, I felt that the finest thing in the world was to be a writer. Except that writing—as a vocation—was too good for us, too good for the mere human being. "Read C. S. Forester so you'll be ready for Melville," my dad told me when I was eight. "Horatio Hornblower before *Moby-Dick*." The implication was that there was a serious apprenticeship, even for reading, to say nothing of the one for writing, and that to presume to write something down took an enormous leap of both faith and pride. (Pride, as most of us with a Christian up-bringing remember, is the first and foremost deadly sin.) So you had to be pure of heart before you started to write, but also full of pride. *Already,* before you wrote the first *the,* you were screwed by your own unworthiness.

When my dad began to write at a big old oak desk he'd bought and shoved into the immaculateness of my parents' bedroom, my mother would alert me. "Come on, Penny! Mr. Big Man's about to start."

My dad would hunch over his typewriter in the corner of that room. My mom and I would sit up on the white chenille bedspread while she kept up that steady, discouraging patter. I was little—five or six or seven—and I was under the dim impression that we were having fun, just as when my mother persuaded me to write "My Daddy is out of shape and has big ears" on the sidewalk outside our house. It was just a joke!

My dad wrote and published six Western pulp stories, stored up his anger, left my mother, and broke her heart. But she'd put a hex on him. He didn't write anything of significance for more than thirty years. Because no matter what "Mr. Big Man" said or thought, Mother knew damn well he wasn't a writer; she knew it the way you know black purses don't go with brown shoes. And my dad was many things, but he was not a dummy. Out of all the women in the world, he'd picked one who knew in her bones—her bone *marrow*—that he didn't have it in him to write. At some level he must have agreed with her.

—

Flash-forward thirty years or so. I'm an associate professor of English (with those two little kids) at Loyola Marymount University. It's parents' day, and I'm sitting in my office telling every last parent that her kids are perfectly fine, and it's a pleasure to teach them.

I'm feeling pretty good. I'm still under forty, I have quantities of long straight blond hair streaming down my back, I have a great pair of purple suede boots, I've—miraculously!—been able to scratch out a partial living as a writer. I've published two books, written an average of one piece a month for a national magazine (some of them turkeys, like *Fitness Today;* some pretty fancy, like *Esquire* and *The Atlantic Monthly*).

A mother and father are sitting in my office, careworn. "We're so worried about Herbert," the mom whispers.

"But he's wonderful! He's a wonderful kid! This is the third class I've had him in, and he's pulled straight A's."

"Well, English . . ." the dad says deprecatingly.

"No, those are *hard* classes! A lot of reading. And he's a wonderful writer, too. He's got a lovely prose style . . ."

The parents look ill. "His brother's in law school," the mom says.

"His sister's a nun," the dad adds somberly.

"Well," I say. "Herb's just a kid. He's only nineteen. He's got plenty of time to decide what he wants to do."

"We're afraid," the mom whispers.

"What is it?"

"We're afraid he wants to be a writer."

They couldn't have been more distressed if he'd told the assembled family at Thanksgiving dinner that he wanted to pursue a career as a boy whore in Calcutta. Their shame is so palpable, so sincere and honest, that—of course—I catch it.

That blond hair I have is helped out by a bottle. Those purple suede boots—I got them on sale, because no one in her right mind would own such a thing: I've never seen another pair like them. My first novel sold under two thousand copies and was scathingly dismissed in the "Books in Brief" column in *The New York Times Book Review.* I'll be forty in a couple of years!

"Well," I mutter. "It's not so bad. There are worse ways . . ."

Mr. Big Man.

———

How I wish this were a made-up story. But it's not. The truth is that about 97 percent of "normal" people everywhere—not just in America—look on writing, if they look on it at all, as one step below whoredom. Because at least if you're a whore you're helping someone have a good time.

It's better to try to be a sculptor, because your mother can show her friends a big chunk of rock out in the backyard and say, "Philip's been working on this since November."

It's better to try and be a stand-up comedian, because your friends can come and watch you bomb out, and there you are sweating, up against a brick wall, but at least you're doing it; it really is you.

It's even better to go west to try and be a movie star, because you can send your folks flimsy little flyers from this little theater or that; or there you are on television dancing around as the dirty underwear in a detergent commercial, and if you achieve even moderate success in even the worst movies, they'll all be watching you back home with loyalty, validation, and envy.

At least they *know* what you're doing when you embark on those crackbrained schemes. But they can't see you write. They don't know what you're doing, and even if you do "succeed"—publish some magazine pieces, or your first or second or third book—relatives will say suspiciously, "I went into the bookstore and asked for your book and they never heard of you." Or, more to the point, "Yes, but how do you make a living?"

Maybe jazz sidemen have as hard a time as writers do, but they can always pull out their trombone and wave it at their aunts and uncles: "*This* is what I play. *This!*"

And, of course, there's the fear your family feels, obsessing in the night about whether or not you're going to write about the time years ago when Dad tried to molest that squirrel but the squirrel would have none of it.

These are just the normal people I'm talking about here, the un-ruling classes, the honest wives and businessmen, the professional hard workers. Even the traditional fuckups— your younger brothers lying around on the couch—are more respectable than you. The jobs they don't have would be *decent* jobs, if they had them. They wouldn't sit for hours in front of a computer drinking coffee, or bad red wine, and just staring.

Maybe you can ignore this shame and disbelief. But it will sap your strength and energy and faith, like taking Bruce Lee's best punch over and over again. So it's best to hang around people who support your work or, at the very least, steer somewhat clear of the people who don't.

———

Take a good look around. There are going to be certain things you need, and there are people around you who need certain things from you.

Do they need for you to be something other than a writer? And if they do, will you be able to stand that? (I'm fairly sure that "Herbert," the boy in my class at Loyola so long ago, did something else with his life. His parents' shame was just too blistering.)

—

Here's the supreme advantage of hanging out with people who don't support your writing. You won't have to write! Or if you do, you won't have to enjoy it. You can pout full-time, look out the window, waste your life, and blame someone else. But that's a colossal bore.

What does "someone who will support your writing" mean?

Let's look at the negatives first. Let's see what it doesn't mean.

People who resent the thought of your writing: They're working hard; you're not.

People who need you to make some money for them. I don't want to be disloyal to my gender, but many women really need men to be "good providers," to be respectable, to allow them to stay home and raise the kids.

People who need you to stay in the background, to be dim and dull so that they can look good. "Pretty" sisters need "smart" sisters, "smart" sisters need "dumb" sisters. Good gardeners need other people to *not* have a green thumb (unless they're generous and evolved).

People who need you to not have "enough," so that whatever they have will look like more.

People who have such a strong idea of what or who you are in *their* universe that they can't begin to see or perceive this other idea you might have about yourself.

You know what? I could go on for five more pages about the people who need you *not* to be a writer. But you get the idea. And they're perfectly okay. They're just working through life on their own agenda. Again, you're going to lose time and energy if you denounce them or rebel against them or defy them.

The smart thing is to be polite and respectful and then gradually fade from view.

—

Who are some of the people who might support your work?

Oddly enough, the least promising place to look for them might be within your town's grungy little enclave of folks with black turtleneck sweaters and bad hair. Lots of them—what we used to call bohemians—have an enormous stake in suffering, or at least looking like they're suffering. They want to be "misunderstood" artists more than they want to be artists, and a large amount of their creativity is apt to be given over to finding reasons why they—and other "serious" writers, artists, painters, poets, etc.—must fail.

Every explanation they give for this sorry state of affairs is absolutely "right": If you publish in a literary magazine, nobody will read you; slick publications hardly ever run short stories; American publishers have merged and merged until there are really only two big ones left; illiteracy is rising; editors only publish the people they know. And so on and so forth.

The lack of support comes not only from philistines or your blushing family or the black-clad sourpusses down at the local coffeehouse. What if you've pulled yourself together and gotten into a creative writing class, or even an MFA program? I don't want to be paranoid here, but it may *look* as if you all want the same thing when in reality you don't. Turn the tables for a minute: How willing are you for *them* to succeed beyond their wildest dreams? How generous is *your* agenda? Those smart, earnest, hardworking young writers may be looking for their own success and no one else's.

And your teachers, I hate to say it, may be sad and disappointed would-be writers seeking to construct a narrative that will justify their own dashed dreams.

Hang out with people who are willing to support your work.

That doesn't mean listening to some chump with a bad bottle of wine who says: "*I* have a good idea! Let's make poetry! I'll write it, you type it, edit it, print off a bunch of copies, and send it out! You get to sleep with me too!" I know a woman whose boyfriend said to her, "I'm married to my poetry, but you can be my mistress." She went for it. And he had hair growing out of his ears, besides!

The proper answer to a remark like that, I guess, is, "Well, yes, I'm married to my work too, but you can be my boy-toy. Do you have any stamps I can borrow? Is your printer working?"

—

I think, in the long run, that to find people who support your work, it's best not even to think in literary terms but to look for easygoing and open-hearted human beings with a low threshold of embarrassment, who, generally speaking, aren't beset by terror, fear, or what we, out here in California, call a "scarcity consciousness."

These are people who think there might be enough of everything for everyone, who can consider popcorn for dinner if you're busy working. You're looking for someone who loves you—or likes you well enough—to let you alone. To say, "*congratulations!*" if you get something published. Someone who doesn't mind if you speak up at parties. (But don't go looking for martyrs to *your* cause, either! Because long-suffering martyrs flare up every once in a while; they get sick of the whole charade, and you can't blame them.)

—

I'm going to talk again about the people in my life—not because my life is anything special, but because it's typical.

My mother was deeply ashamed of my writing until I could buy a house. Then she was a good sport about it, getting me gigs in her neighborhood library, coming with me on tour a couple of times.

My dad, who I always thought would support me in my efforts, was deeply offended when I began to make a living writing. He had always taken the position that our family had suffered too much to actually succeed. (He changed his tune when he found his métier late in life.)

My first husband, an elegant, brokenhearted artiste, knew for a fact that if you were smart enough to want to write, you were also smart enough to realize the extent of your own mediocrity. All of us had "second-rate minds"; wasn't it terrible? That rascal! He ended up being the hero of one of my novels and a character in one of Alison Lurie's novels and a major character in my daughter Lisa See's nonfiction book *On Gold Mountain* and then a character in the opera that came from that, and even as I write, there's a *five-year exhibit* over at the children's section of the Autry Museum here in Los Angeles that has to do with Richard's seventh birthday party. Think of it! That guy's been used more in contemporary American culture than a piece of hotel soap, and he's never had to write a word.

My second husband supported my writing except when I wrote. Then he took it badly. He felt swindled and betrayed, because he'd always wanted to write. It got bad, what with my one thousand words a day and vengeful disposition. It wasn't going to work out, and it didn't.

If you want to write, you have to pay attention and *look for what you want.* For twenty-seven years, until he died, I lived with John Espey, a kind scholar and writer, who was happy when I was happy and who was proud of my work. I began to notice couples like Joan Didion and John Gregory Dunne, who didn't compete; they strengthened each other, and the two of them were far stronger than just one writer. They were the Didion-Dunnes! (Your partner doesn't have to be a writer, just a best friend who loves you.)

As my daughters grew up, Lisa began to write and the two of us were pestered with questions—separately: "How do you, uhm, *feel* about your mother/daughter, *writing*? And she even has the same last name as you?" The truth is, I think we feel fine. And my younger daughter, who always said she was "not a writer," is writing for a newspaper.

Roger Simon, a fine mystery writer, once gave a wonderful speech, in which he said: The success of any of your friends is a genuine cause for rejoicing, because it brings you closer to the charmed circle of people who are doing their best work and having a good time.

It goes without saying that if you're looking for someone to support you in your most tender dreams, you'd better be at least moderately willing to support that person as well.

—

When she was in a bad mood, my mother used to dance around and say, "You've got to take shit, take shit, take *shit*!" I disagreed with her on principle, but it's true that there are barnacles on every yacht, that about 50 percent of everything we ever do is boring shit-work. For every expedition to the South Pole, there are months, years, that the explorers put in fund-raising, recruiting, shopping for supplies, balancing the budget. For every public office, pounds of hotel chicken are eaten, bad speeches are given and heard. Every radiant baby produces a mountain of dirty diapers.

The writing life carries with it a huge amount of junk (mailing those envelopes; making those phone calls; keeping track of all your receipts for the tax man; addressing invitations to signings).

Can you get past the idyllic picture of yourself alone at your desk? Can you consider some of the dirty work? Would you do some of that work for somebody else; would he or she do some of it for you? Would you consider hanging out with people who support your work? *And vice versa?*

If it seems like too much to ask of your family and friends, maybe you want to back off. Or consider very delicately shifting around the relationships in your family. Getting yourself a better set of friends.

Chapter 7

Do Some Magic

People who are riding high don't need magic; they're riding high already. But some of the rest of us do. Paramahansa Yogananda—who wrote the charming classic *Autobiography of a Yogi*—devotes an entire chapter to his youth in an India that was crawling with yogis with time on their hands—the Out Crowd of swamis. There was the Perfume Swami, who'd pester Yogananda: "What's your favorite perfume?"

Yogananda would answer, "I don't have a favorite perfume, I'm a guy. Besides, I'm on the way to school here."

"No, but really, what's your favorite perfume?"

"I don't like perfume."

"But if you did like perfume, what kind would it be?"

And Yogananda, exasperated beyond words, would finally say, "Jasmine, all right?" And keep on walking.

But the Perfume Swami would tag right along with him, rubbing his hands together, and finally wave one under Yogananda's nose, saying, "Smell *that*? Just tell me what it is!"

And Yogananda, ducking into the school yard, would have to concede wearily, "Jasmine. Very nice."

Going home from school, he'd try to avoid the Two Place Swami, who'd be languidly leaning against a fence, just so he could wave his hand and say, "Hi there, Paramahansa!" and Yogananda would politely acknowledge his greeting, only to be accosted once again at the end of the block by the Two Place Swami: "Hi there!" And Yogananda would duck his head and scurry home, because no matter how many places he managed to be in, the Two Place Swami was always a bit of a bore.

There are several ways to look at these stories. Couldn't those guys find something better to do with their power than conjure up some lousy perfume? Or, if you're a bore in one place, there's absolutely no reason to think you'll be anything else in *two* places!

You can choose to think that Paramahansa Yogananda was making it all up, that each and every "supernatural" manifestation was and is a trick. But magic, emotions, miracles, the occult, the weird, the bizarre, and the unaccountable belong to the world of the imagination. For instance, in the first years after Christ, the Romans lived very well. They had aqueducts and temples and soldiers with fancy armor and wide roads and nice pottery and imposing statuary, and they had an okay religion, which they didn't follow very religiously, because who needed it? Things were going fine.

But meanwhile, just across the Mediterranean, the early Christians were going ape crazy. They were mesmerized, inspired, *wired* by the memory of a guy who, besides preaching divine love and the forgiveness of sin, would have put any Two

Place Swami to shame. He walked on water. He fed a huge crowd on a couple of loaves and fishes. He raised folks from the dead. He cured the sick. And maybe most telling of all, he changed jar after jar of water into wine—*excellent* wine—so that the people at Cana may have come expecting the dull wedding of a couple living in modest circumstances but came away from a party that will be remembered as long as there are Christians.

Two things are evident from this: one, the early Christians, poor, obscure, and marginalized as they were, had a lot of fun; two, you don't see too many people around nowadays who worship Zeus.

———

Miracles, white magic, enthusiasm are fun to play with. Maybe we can't be in two places at once or cure the sick and raise the dead. But we can make a crying child laugh through her tears or turn a mess of white beans and ham hocks into a perfect meal or reverse a dying relationship with a crash program of smiles, compliments, and sex. We can play the devil, too. (Ever give in to temptation and say to someone who'd been having a nice day up until then, "You must have put on your lipstick with a butter knife!" These are hexes, mere words, but they have the power to cripple for a good long time, maybe for life.)

This may be the chapter you won't want to read or the one you won't want to "believe" in. But at least you'll still have your "common sense" dignity: You won't be staring at some fish and a slice of bread saying, "Multiply, won't you *please*? Just be a sport and multiply!"

———

How about doing some *affirmations*? What if you look in the mirror first thing in the morning and suggest, "I am a powerful, loving, and creative being, and I can handle it, and I can have anything I want!" Then say it again. And again. Or, "I deserve the very best, and now is the time for it!" Or, "My income increases daily whether I'm working, playing, or sleeping." Or, "Money comes to me now, in expected and unexpected ways!" Or, my personal favorite, "Everything always turns out for me, more exquisitely than I ever planned."

Oh, no, no, no! How weird is *this*? What are we in, some kind of Dale Carnegie insane asylum for aspiring writers?

Actually, affirmations come straight out of the nineteenth-century American Midwest, from a respectable religious movement called New Thought. Disfranchised farmers managed to turn their lives around, at least somewhat, by this particular aspect of "positive thinking." Does it "work"? How should I know? But what it does for writers is this: Affirmations make a nice counterpart to the other wretched noise that gets turned up in your brain when you write, or even think about writing: "Look at Mr. Big Man!"

"Carolyn See isn't half the writer she thinks she is," Dwight Macdonald wrote about me in *Playboy* years ago, and there it still is, in stunning black-and-white. That's why it's nice to remember that "I'm powerful, loving, and creative."

These voices aren't always personal. "Forget about being published. You're learning the art of the short story for the love of it. Nobody publishes short stories!" I've heard this many more times than I like to remember from reputable writing teachers with good hearts who want to save their students from rejection.

"Everybody's seen it; nobody wants it," my own very sweet editor said to me about the (then nonexistent) paperback of my memoir, *Dreaming*. *"Everybody's seen it; nobody wants it."* Yikes! Ow! *The pain!* It's a good thing I remembered that "I deserve the very best and now is the time for it" and thus got up the courage to call a friend of mine at a university press. The paperback is still in print, doing very nicely, thank God.

"There's no room for mid-list fiction anymore."

"The whole publishing business is owned by people who don't care about literature!"

"If they don't like you, that's it!"

"All the smaller houses are gone."

In other words, why write? Everybody will see it; nobody will want it. You probably aren't half the writer you think you are.

That's why it's nice to reassure your timid, frightened brain that *you deserve the very best and now is the time for it. That you're a powerful, loving, and creative person and you can have anything you want. That you're perfectly happy and satisfied, right now in this moment!* That even when your relatives tell you that you can't make a living from writing, you can say to yourself (and even to *them* if you feel like it), "Money comes to me now in expected and unexpected ways," or, "My income increases daily whether I'm working, playing, or sleeping."

Does this magic "work"? Again, I don't know. I do know it takes you out of this world and into the mystical one, where life is fun and anything can happen; where, when you drive the car, you can say out loud, "I feel like a success; I *am* a success" and see what will happen next, wait for your life to unfold with a sense of pleasure and surprise. And don't forget: "I always drive in perfect safety," and, "I always find a safe, easy, and convenient parking place." (More fun than "I can't stand this fucking traffic. Get out of the *way,* you asshole!" and other negative affirmations that interfere with your peace of mind and the quality of your life.)

—

I can't tell you how many times my writing students have said to me, "I can't do dialogue." Or, "I have so much trouble with plot!" Or, "I don't know what to put into this story and what to cut. I can't seem to figure out what's important."

I say to them, "How about if you *could* do dialogue?" Or, "You *have* the perfect plot, right there in your brain." Or, "You're a perfect editor; you just don't know it yet."

They don't buy it; they *can't* buy it. So I suggest they say, out loud, in the car, at home, "*Up until now,* I couldn't do dialogue, but now I love it! I can't wait to type in those quotation marks and see what my characters have to say!" And, "*Up until now,* I had some trouble with plot, but now it's my greatest strength. I'm a fiend for plot!" And, "My natural good taste and fine subconscious mind naturally know what to put in and what to cut out of a story."

Why is it so easy to believe the awful and never to believe the good?

I have two affirmations that I'm crazy about:

My ideas come faster than I can write, and they're all good ideas.

And the other one:

> I see it!
> I feel it!
> I know it!
> I *got* it!

This works. It's a powerful spiritual exercise, a meditation. Repeated twenty to fifty times, it does something to the brain. It banishes fear and brings inspiration.

—

Affirmations are magic to the ear, but you can work with other senses as well. There's nothing that says you can't make pictures of what you'll eventually do, be, and have. Why not start with a coat of arms. Here's mine.

FUN first!

My goodness me; what about *love*? I say fun first, and this is why: My dad left my mom. My first two husbands and I had many maudlin arguments over the question of who loved whom when. I've thought long and hard about this question. My father had the golden knack of making fun wherever he went. I had a lot of fun with my first two husbands before (and, miraculously, after) our divorces. I never want to be in a position in my life where some beloved can tell me, "I never loved you," and have that break my heart again. I take the aikido position: "Yeah, but we did have a lot of fun." It's complimentary to all, makes no one a villain, minimizes heartbreak.

So I go for fun first, then love.

Then fame, then money.

Fun	Love
Fame	$

I don't mean a lot of fame. A "serious" novelist, with a very few exceptions, isn't going to get much of that. (But once, when I went into Weight Watchers, the cashier recognized my name.) I'd like to be remembered, by at least a few people, for at least a little while. The money isn't that important to me, but it's important enough to get on the coat of arms, and by this point I can call myself a prosperous matron and be proud of it, since I've made my living by my pen.

But when I spoke to a workshop run by Betty Friedan and I'd put this diagram on the board, talking about priorities, and how you could map your life, she pitched a fit. "What about social justice! What about service to the community? What about compassion! What about improving the world?"

Of course I cared about those things. But I didn't feel like altering my diagram. I stared at the blackboard, stupefied. Then a man at the back of the class stood up, came down the aisle, took the chalk from my hand. "Let me," he said, and drew a heart, so that it looked like this:

Fun	Love
Fame	$

"Everything you do is in the context of affection, social justice, and bettering humanity. How about that?"

It felt better. It looked better, too. It reminds me to tithe, for one thing, to give 10 percent of all I earn to the charities of my choice. It reminds me that I've got larger things to think about than myself, or even my "art."

What I'm suggesting is that you play around with this stuff. It isn't new. Nike has its swoosh; Richard the Lionhearted had his lion. What do you have? Love of the wilderness? Of women? Fast cars? Deep-sea fishing? Conquering the world? This is something for you to do while you're at some boring job talking on the phone. Draw on a notepad. It's the tagger impulse. It's a way of knowing you're alive. Magic.

—

In the privacy of your own home—or with people you absolutely love and trust—why not make some treasure maps? Draw pictures of what you want and need in this literary life of yours. If you're working on a book, what's the title? Write it out nicely, on a good sheet of paper. Be sure to put your name on as the author.

What's that cover going to be like? Authors are always bitching and moaning about the terrible covers their publishers have stuck them with. Well, now's your chance. Draw the cover. If you've got some pastels or crayons around, you can block in some color. Good! Because if you can't envision it, you can't have it. (Think of all the Italians before Christopher Columbus who never made it to America because they couldn't imagine it was there!) But now, in however rough a form, here's a visual manifestation of your book—that's in addition to the steadily growing manuscript that you print out every day.

Suppose you leave a white strip at the bottom of the cover? That's where you put in blurbs from your favorite critics, give yourself a rave from *The New York Times* ("A wondrous piece of unparalleled genius!"—Michiko Kakutani, *The New York Times*). If you're feeling especially brave, you might want to clip *The New York Times* Best-Seller List and type in your book, your name—your *work*—in the place where it belongs. (Sadly enough, I could never get myself any farther up the list than number 7, even when I was all alone in the house with scissors, paper, and glue.)

Of course there are other ways to use treasure maps: Go to a car dealer, come home with a glossy brochure, cut out a picture of your favorite model, find a handsome photograph of yourself, glue it in where the driver is sitting, caption it with a perky affirmation: "Edward fully enjoys his Porsche 911; he drives in perfect safety and has no trouble at all with the payments."

I know women who find an anorexic model, cut out her image, paste her up on a piece of paper, cut out their own face, paste *that* on with accompanying text: "Jacqueline absolutely enjoys weighing in at an average of ninety-five pounds and is *happy* subsisting on a diet of melons!" "Thin" treasure maps have never worked for me—never! Not at my most manic and "creative"—because my love of chicken-fried steak and quesadillas far outweighs my wavering wish to be thin.

But that hasn't kept me from putting together "travel" treasure maps—China and Australia or Bali or Singapore—featuring the Forbidden City or Ayers Rock or wonderful pictures of lounge singers at Raffles Hotel, with cutout pictures of my sweet friend John Espey and me and some kind of caption: "Carolyn and John love their time spent at Uluru: Australia loves them and they love Australia!" I write out a check to myself for five thousand dollars or so and stick it on the map to remind myself that no matter how broke we are, we'll always have the money to go on great trips, because that's the kind of people we are.

It works. How? The "grown-up" interpretation might be that if you expend the energy to make them, think about them, and stick them up on a wall where you can see them every day, affirmations function as a psychological reminder, a contract with yourself. The interpretation I prefer is this: They work because they *work;* that's all. Do we spend time quibbling about how a fax functions, or an internal combustion engine or our computer? No. We send the fax, start the car, log on.

—

Remember to "outflow." Hemingway said, we never truly possess something unless we have given it away. Christ said, cast your bread upon the waters and it will return to you. Any philanthropist knows that the more money he gives, the more he'll get back; any volunteer knows that hours spent in a good cause give us golden time. We all know, at some level, that stinginess doesn't work.

If you start giving away that which you want, you give the universe a nudge—you get the cosmic Jell-O trembling.

Suppose you're a mom with three little kids. What would happen if three times a week you phoned a friend to say, "Why don't you drop your kids off here for the afternoon. You look like you could use the time!" Or what if you astonished your husband as he skulks around the house on a Saturday morning thinking how he can pick a fight and get out of the house so he can play some golf by this: "Honey, you work so hard! You need some time for yourself. Is it too late to go play some golf?" (Looked at one way, you're a martyr who's taken leave of your senses. Looked at in another—better—way, you're a philanthropist of time. And by the laws of the ever-expanding universe, "Whatever you spend comes back to you vastly multiplied, and that's okay!")

The way to be rich is to give away your money, and the more broke you are, the more essential it is: to pay the fare of the person behind you at the toll booth, to leave the two quarters in the well of the pay phone, to find the charities you like and lay money on them. Not out of virtue, but to stir things up, get the universe moving.

If you're stone-broke and totally discouraged, donate your old clothes, give someone a ride to school, baby-sit free. You're never so wretched that you can't give something away.

If you feel like you don't have enough love in your life (no writer, artist, human being can exist without love), don't go around trying to steal it at low bars from impressionable young men and women: Try *giving it away,* in a blaze of affection, compliments, and hugs. Start with your musty old grandma, your lumpy wife, your doltish dad: hugs and compliments—because you have so much love in your bank that you can afford to give it away, lavishly and recklessly.

You're not doing this to be "good" or to get to heaven on the fast track. You're doing this to draw designs in the universe, casting your bread on the edge of the pond, watching it go on out there and eddy on back in again, practicing the magic of outflow, looking to become a millionaire in work and love.

—

There's a chance that all this advice will make you faintly sick—because you're not "the kind of person" who goes around doing silly stuff. If you have only one thing, you have that dignity of yours. Or your "integrity." Or your timidity. Or your terror of rejection. So you couldn't even think of doing any of this, because it would mess too much with the kind of person you *are*.

But haven't you had a hand in creating the person you are? Sure, your parents were in on it ("Ted's the athlete, Bob's the smart one, and Jerry's never going to get a decent job if he doesn't get off the couch and make something of himself!"). But you can bet that Ted's working out pretty regularly, Bob's doing his homework, and Jerry's probably eating barbecue potato chips because he likes them. By the time we're six or seven, we've already reached an implicit agreement with the universe about the kind of people we are.

Think about the things that put you on the moral high ground. If you're dead set against fast food or red meat or oral sex or shaving your legs or hard liquor or bad language, you might want to go ahead and give some of that a shot. Just to see what it feels like.

—

The other day, on the UCLA campus during finals week, I saw a student of mine stretched out on the grass under a tree, looking up at the leaves. It was finals week! All around us, students and faculty were scurrying from there to here and here to there looking purposeful and worried. This was important! This was a time that was full of stress!

I stopped near my student and looked down.

"Donald! What's up?"

Without moving a lick, he looked over at me.

"I'm creating the now," he said.

"Well," said I. "Keep up the good work!"

That's it, isn't it? Do we cry, or do we go out sailing? Do we eat dog food when we're poor and old, or do we make gourmet carrot soup? Do we sit on the couch or go out for a walk? Do we fall in love or make some poor bastard's life a living hell? Do we look out the window and groan about our wasted life, or do we make a plan to see if we can live our dream? Do we go through life asleep or try to wake up?

I hope I'm wrong, but I imagine that about 90 percent of the human race is snoozing along, just going through the motions. And 100 percent of us dull out some of the time. It takes miracles, white magic, wonders, to jog us from our slumber. What if we really were masters of our mind and life? What if we were God-in-action? What would we do then?

Everything we write is some kind of answer to that question.

Chapter 8

Make Rejection a Process

You've finished a twelve-page story. You've played with it and revised it and looked at it. (You have a shade of a sick feeling that there might be something wrong with it, but that might be a standard case of nerves or an even more standard case of self-loathing.) You've given copies of it to your friends to read (even though that's a bad idea) and they've said— falsely? kindly?—"It's great, it really is. No, I don't see anything wrong with it. Why don't you send it out? You've got a real gift there. No, really."

You give it to your lover or sweetheart. He or she says, "It seems wonderful to me. Because everything you do is wonderful."

And, of course, if you present your twelve pages to a workshop and after you've read them, they just *stare* at you, as uncomprehendingly as lizards—well, what do *they* know? They're assholes, every one of them!

The truth is: You can't believe what your friends, lovers, or enemies say. Even if what they say is the God's honest truth, it doesn't matter, because they're not going to be able to buy your work and print it or, conversely, keep it from being bought and printed.

So you send it out, and between five days and five months later you get it back, in your self-addressed manila envelope, with a snotty little printed note: *Sorry, this does not meet our needs at this time.* Sometimes it's signed and sometimes it isn't. You look at it, scan it for clues. *Sorry, this does not meet our needs at this time.* Does it actually mean they don't like it? That your friends and lovers were lying? That your enemies were right? Could it actually mean that you're not any good? That you were fooling yourself all the time? That you don't have a . . . "gift"?

It goes without saying that ever since you saw your own stamped self-addressed manila envelope in the mailbox, you've been suffering the tortures of the damned. It's as if every ion in your body has been reversed; as if you've literally been struck by lightning, as if your liver has ruptured and your spleen's been set afire and your vision has blurred—is it just tears or a brain tumor? It's going to last, this ghastly, terrible, unspeakable rejection, from a period of about two hours to the rest of your life.

I wish I were exaggerating, but I'm not. I can't tell you the number of workshops, signings, seminars, etc., where some haggard person takes hold of my hand, looks into my eyes, and says, "*I* used to want to be a writer. And I sent out a story. I never heard back from them—never." If I'm churl enough to inquire if they ever wrote a follow-up letter to ask what happened to the story, they gaze at me with the eyes of a beaten dog. They sent out a story and never heard anything about it again!

You hear stories about misunderstood writers collecting their cold, impersonal, fiendishly mean rejection slips and tacking them up on the wall just over their desks: *That* must be an encouraging sight every morning when they sit down to write! Sometimes the pain of rejection is so horrible that it overwhelms the pleasure of writing. So you scale down your dreams or give up on them altogether.

—

There's a better way. Remember the hypothesis that life (and writing) are like courtship, romance, even sex? Instead of thinking of rejection as a life-blighting event, make it into a dating game.

What if you were a nice-looking woman of childbearing age walking down the street minding your own business when a slightly shifty man—or woman—walked up behind you and said, "Wanna fuck?" The chances are 50 million to one that you'd say no. You'd start running, you'd yell for the police, you'd rush to your car and drive away. If you had all kinds of politesse and control, you might be able to mutter, "No thank you," but that wouldn't change your essential response: *Sorry, this does not meet my needs at this time!*

This is not as far-fetched as it seems. The person doing the wooing, such as it is, often has a far different idea of what's going on than the one being wooed.

Now, suppose you're a guy and you see a woman who looks kind of cute. In fact, she looks great! And you hear her talking, maybe, and she's got a nice laugh. What you'd really like, more than anything else you can think of, is to nab her. It's not just the sex you want—you can pay a prostitute for that (that's called "vanity publishing"). You think you might want the whole package. It's worth putting some thought and imagination into the courtship process. Because if you just walked up to her and said, out of the blue, "Wanna fuck?" of course, she'd say *no!*

So you ask her out for coffee. Take her to a couple of movies. Haul her out to the beach—if there's a shoreline anywhere around—and tell her your life story. Take an interest when she tells you hers. Pull out some amusing conversation if you have any. In my life, I've discovered the really successful seducers are the ones who don't nag or pout or bully. They take the position that the magic afternoons both of you are thinking about are already a *done deal.* You're lovers *already,* sparring and bantering, playing around, having fun. It's only a matter of time until you get into bed. It's up to the one being courted to decide when that happens, and the successful seducer is willing—*more* than willing!—for it to take as long as it takes.

To radically shift metaphors for a paragraph, editors, playing "hard to get" at every level, are programmed to act like those plastic ducks you used to see in 99-cent stores. Their little heads with their pink bills are set to wag back and forth: *no, no, no, no, no.* But the thing about those ducks was: With timing and concentration, you could put a drop of water on their bills, and from then on they'd nod *yes, yes, yes, yes, yes!* How do you get the duck to do that? It's certainly possible; it's part of the game.

Rejection is a process, not an event. You, for instance, envision yourself in the pages of a particular periodical. The people at that periodical don't share your fantasy. If they were that nice-looking woman of childbearing age, they'd be walking down the street minding their own business. You're a stranger to them (unless by lucky chance you've met them). They've never heard of you.

So you send them a manuscript, and they send it back. Believe me, if you were Jesus Christ himself, they'd send it back. Because they've never met you!

Here's what you do: In that first hour of rejection, when your liver is exploding and your spleen is on fire, you grope your way through the house to where you keep your "charming note" stationery. You look up the name of that periodical's editor on the masthead and you write him or her a charming note.

You don't, under any circumstances, write: "Dear Sir or Madam, Eat shit and die." (Would you do that if you were out walking on the beach with a cute girl and she refused your first offer?)

Try writing something like "Thanks for the bracing experience of your rejection slip! It made me rethink my story once again. I'll be sending you another one in three weeks or so. Because my greatest dream is to see my work in your pages. Maybe next time I'll get a genuine signature on that slip! Or maybe you'll say yes. Wouldn't that be cool? Yours sincerely."

Write it, fold it, address it, stamp it, send it right back *on the same day you get the rejection.*

I can't tell you how important this is, how utterly unfrivolous in intent. This simple *thank you* for the rejection is one of the highest forms of spiritual aikido I can think of. Editors aren't dumb. They're perfectly aware that within this "rejection" exchange they hold all the power. They may even send your manuscript hurtling back with a certain sour joy, but you take that freaky energy and post it instantly back *to them.*

Maybe they'll read the note and drop it instantly into the wastebasket. Maybe they'll shove it to the back of their desks. It doesn't matter too much what *they* do.

The main thing is that *your* ions will fall back into place, your internal organs will stop exploding, and you might find yourself absently smiling. Instead of waking in the night in a ghastly sweat quoting the dreaded *Sorry, this does not meet our needs at this time,* you may start obsessing along the lines of *Thanks for the bracing experience!* Maybe next time it should be *Many thanks for the bracing experience!* Or, *If adversity builds character, my character got a big boost from your bracing rejection! I'll send you another piece soon.* Or, simply and weirdly, the kind of thing that will wake *them* at night with a chilly jolt, a card—embossed, if you can afford it, on matte card paper—that says *Thank you.* With your signature. And a line in your own handwriting underneath: *Maybe next time?*

Sometimes my students, cringing at the very thought, say, "Won't that make them mad?" But what's to get upset about?

It's just a thank-you note. The only real message it sends is *I'm not dead, thank you very much!*

These notes carry great strength. They introduce the element of surprise into the rejection/acceptance process. Many years ago, I had it in my mind that it would be a great thing to be published by *The Atlantic Monthly.* I was still playing by the East Coast rules. If I'd given it a moment's rational thought, I would have realized that the last thing on earth a Boston-based, male-dominated, utterly dignified magazine would want or need would be the semi-hysterical, heartbroken howlings of a West Coast divorcée. I didn't realize it, though. I kept sending them things—sending them and sending them—to a kind but strict man named C. Michael Curtis, who finally got fed up and wrote something to me like: "Dear Miss See, I think that by now you've sent us everything but your family photograph album. I should think it would be evident that we're not interested in the kind of things you write."

I cried and kicked the walls, but when I calmed down I sent him a handful of photographs—of me and my then-grubby kids living a raffish life in the wilds of Topanga Canyon with our own tram line, switchback path, goat, chickens, etc. *Not dead yet, thank you very much!*

He sent them back with a weak "Very funny, Carolyn," and that was that, until a few months later, when I found myself in Boston, made an appointment with him, and he gave me an assignment—because he *knew* me—which later got a literary award. (To be honest, that whole issue of the magazine got the award, but I got to go to New York and someone gave me a diploma.) Twenty years later I saw Mike Curtis at a writers' conference and reminded him of our exchange. He didn't remember, because he *certainly* isn't the kind of person to ever be swayed by a handful of photos of a divorced mom, a couple of children, and a goat. Except, he was.

—

To move a little further in the process, there is no better cure for a bad *review* than a thank-you note. There's probably no worse rejection in the world than a bad review of a book you've cherished and loved into existence over a period of three, five, ten years. My mother recently died not speaking to me on her deathbed, and that was a mere bee sting compared to what Martin Levin wrote about my poor little first novel in a "Books in Brief" review in *The New York Times Book Review.*

Writing that last paragraph, I have to think, *why?* Why did Martin Levin's rejection hurt worse than my mother's last act? Because I was sitting by her bed, saying civil things. *I held up my end of the transaction,* and ultimately it was her business what she took into the next world with her. But Martin Levin's attack came out of the blue. I felt powerless to do anything about it. At the time I suffered greatly.

But you can control how much you suffer. Think of it, again, as spiritual aikido. What book critics do (and I speak as one) when they write a bad review is hurl a tremendously destructive object that can either be a spear or a boomerang. Usually, it's a spear. The author takes the bad review literally to heart, lies down on his or her bed and bleeds for a year or two.

But sometimes it works another way. The author reaches up, gives the spear a graceful twist. The lethal weapon goes hurtling back to the book reviewer's desk with a startling and unnerving *whoosh*. Jerzy Kosinski once sent me a beautifully polite thank-you note for a bad review I gave him, and I was afraid to go out of the house for a week: He knew where I lived, in more ways than one.

A lady who was once married to Salman Rushdie had one of her novels published just as the famous fatwa was handed down on him. I gave the book a bad review. I was surprised that her pretty awful novel got a solemn, respectful review in *The New York Times* and everywhere else I looked. I was probably the only literate person in America who hadn't heard about the fatwa, and when I found out, I was sorry for what I had written. The poor woman had enough to worry about. A few years later, she got hold of one of my novels to review for *The Washington Post* and she *killed* me! She said I wrote "embarrassing surfer prose." Oh, the agony!

I sent her a book on surfing, inscribed "It isn't as easy as it looks," and immediately felt much better. Around that time, in the continuing seesaw of rejection/acceptance that ricochets through all literary lives, I left the *Los Angeles Times* and went over to *The Washington Post*.

And though my memoir, *Dreaming: Hard Luck and Good Times in America*, got a lovely review in *The New York Times Book Review*, Michiko Kakutani, the weekday critic for the paper, had a definitely mixed opinion about the same book. The personal stuff was okay, she wrote, but when I ventured opinions about the American government, I was "silly, turgid and presumptuous." Everyone I ever knew in America called me the morning that review came out.

There's a time difference between New York and L.A. of three hours, so by about seven in the morning my time I was answering the phone: "Silly, Turgid and Presumptuous," as though I were a law firm. But by 10 A.M. I'd managed to write a note on my very best stationery: *"Dear Michiko Kakutani, I'd rather be trashed by you than praised by many."* Which is true; she's a very fine critic. But the nice thing about this note was that for the next thirty or so calls, I could answer the phone like a normal person and then say, "Oh yes, I *did* see it. I already wrote her a nice thank-you note."

People want to know sometimes: Did you actually die when they rejected you so cruelly? It's reassuring to everyone to be able to say, "No, *I'm not dead yet, thank you very much.*" And that weird boomerang of energy whooshes around a few more times: rejection, acceptance, praise, rejection, acceptance.

———

Sometimes we have a neurotic, inexplicable need to be re- jected. A way to invite rejection—without the trouble of hav- ing to produce an actual manuscript—is to send off a pathetic query note: "Dear Sir or Madam, I am a student of anthropol- ogy at Bitteroot State University and I am wondering if you'd be interested in an interview with that beautiful girl on *Friends.* I've been a fan of hers for a long time."

Remember that respectable woman of childbearing age, a.k.a. the editor? If you were in your right mind, you'd *know* she'd say no to this, so maybe that's what you're doing: asking for your very own rejection. (I know a man, married to a *real* woman of childbearing age; they have three kids, in fact. He waits until two in the morning, when she's finally asleep, to demand sex. It's when he most craves "release," he says. This method of courtship is a great way to never have sex with your wife and get to say that it's her fault.)

I hate the idea of query notes, because their very form invites editors to say no. You should never write anything to an editor in the form of a question if you can help it. (You want to do everything you can to keep from activating that automatic plastic duck thing.)

Again, it's better to take the position that you're already proceeding from some kind of done deal. Why not try a charming note consisting entirely of declarative sentences? It's no biggie: You're looking at a note that runs nine to twelve lines.

The first paragraph, of three or four lines, indicates who you are and why you always read that particular periodical. "As a working mom, I'm never without my copy of *Parenting*."

Or, "As someone who's been traveling around the world by pushcart for the last three years, I don't make a move without *Outside* magazine."

Or, "As someone plagued by too much intelligence and way too much clinical depression, I look forward each month to *Bleak* more than I can say."

The second paragraph tells what you want to write about: "My baby has been afflicted by projectile vomiting, but I believe—in fact, I *know*—I've found a miracle cure."

Or, "I'm writing this from Thailand, where I've found fellow pushcart aficionados engaging in lucrative jewel smuggling. Frankly, it blew me away!"

Or, "My parents got fed up and had me committed, but I felt better 'inside' than out, to tell you the truth. I've found the best way to survive in rehab without giving up the melancholy that is so essential to the intellectual today."

The third paragraph tells why you're the best person on earth—or at least the best person *they'll* ever find—to write this particular piece of work.

"It's my great-grandmother's remedy from the early nineteenth century, when she was a pioneer traveling by covered wagon from Tennessee to West Texas. Everything old is new again, it turns out."

Or, "Against my better judgment, I got involved in the business and spent six months in a Bangkok jail."

Or, "I've discovered how to participate in a suicide ring and always be the last one chosen."

The last lines are always the same: "I'll be sending something along to you in three or four weeks. I hope you're as excited about it as I am."

Now you can argue about the quality of these notes, but you can't easily figure out how to say no to them. (And why would you want to? Wouldn't anyone want to find the cure for projectile vomiting? Learn what it's like inside a Bangkok jail? Participate in a suicide pact without going through the inconvenience of having to die?)

And although it's not necessarily a good idea to show your *work* to any innocent passersby, sometimes it's good to use a friend to "trade with" as you write these notes. You care deeply about your own career, but you only care about your friend's career in the most benign and detached way. Why don't you write his notes and let him write yours? You're just batting tennis balls against a garage door, sending a literary or journalistic shuttlecock across the cosmic net. If an editor rouses himself from his torpor long enough to write, "No! No nasturtiums, poultices, garnets, or suicide attempts now or *ever*!" you can blame it on your friend, and make him write the thank-you note back, while you do the same for him.

—

A few words about e-mail, and energy.

E-mail is a wonderful thing, and certainly it's grand to fire off a couple of civil e-mails a day to whomever you love and admire, but *be careful!* That SEND is so seductive. If you feel you must write an irate letter, write it on paper and let it sit for a couple of days. Then tear it up and write a civilized one. If you tap out an eat-shit-and-die note on the computer and then click on SEND, that's it. So *be careful.*

—

The energy that accrues around messages is extraordinary, mystical, immeasurable. Jean Anouilh wrote a lovely one-act play about a girl who changed her world by only speaking the words *I love you.* It was a fantasy, of course. But not completely. Instead of rejection, she was dealing in affectionate acceptance.

What we're dealing with—all of us, all the time—is energy. The energy that makes an editor pick up a half-sheet that says

Sorry, but your manuscript does not meet our needs at this time and jam it into a manila envelope headed straight back to you, the opposing energy that you put into a thank-you note.

It's not personal. It's not death. It's just a death experience. And the way to defuse rejection is to turn it into a *process:* cosmic badminton. So that *you* can wake up in the night, think about it, and actually smile.

Chapter 9

Getting Published, Part I

Today I got a swell fax from my agent. "Very good news from France!" it began, and went on to say that a section from my novel *The Handyman* was going to be published in *Elle*. In France. In French. I'd like to be cool about it, but I can't. It just knocks me out that over there on the Métro, elegant Parisian ladies are going to be opening up their copies of *Elle* and there I'll be.

There's the world I was in when I took the car to the shop for a tune-up this morning and was worrying about *not* being invited to a big party that all my friends were going to, but all the time there, on the fax machine, was this message: "Very good news from France!" Another—better—world.

Outside of having children, or dying, nothing more dramatic or life-changing can happen to you than to see your work in print. Oh, maybe winning the U.S. Open or the America's Cup, but I'm not sure about that, because those are fleeting moments, gone almost as soon as they happen. When you have something in print, even if it's a recipe for heirloom tomato aspic, you've bought a ticket in immortality's lottery. Part of you is floating in another universe, and until every last copy of whatever-it-is, is burned, smashed, and gone, you are, because of that little scrap, not bound by the rules of time.

There it is: the two-thousand-word piece on the mating of moles; the love sonnet that actually *sits right there* in the literary quarterly; the short story that shows up—God knows how!—in a women's magazine. The shameless delight that comes from seeing your name in print is incomparable. There's no point in saying "It doesn't matter," because it does matter. In the most powerful way, it proves that you exist and that you have something to say. It's what sets you off from "ordinary people," provides proof of your inner life.

This is when your ego tends to go stark raving mad. And there's no point in saying that you're above these things, because you often don't even *know* you have an ego until you get into print.

You always suspected the world revolved around you, but your mother set you straight. By the time you got to kindergarten you realized there were other kids, that you were just one of many. But now, look! The proof is undeniable: Right there in the newspaper: "Making Love Can Keep You Fit," and there's your name right underneath it! Or there, in the campus magazine: "Adios, Barcelona."

Nothing in the world is going to persuade you that there's anything more important than seeing your name in print—not the Ebola virus or World War Three or the love of your life.

Your ego is a big, messy, undisciplined, anxiety-ridden dog. It barks and whines and pees on the floor and sheds all over the furniture and takes nips at passing strangers and goes *crazy* when it sees another dog that might be bigger or smarter or prettier. This dog—at least in my experience—is untrainable. The only thing you can do is try to keep it on a fairly short leash.

I've seen writers misbehave, and God knows I've misbehaved myself. I've watched distinguished authors show up at conferences only to storm off, saying: "I'm used to *at least* being the keynote speaker!" Or, "I'm not used to being seated *below the salt!*"

And I've seen writers pitch hissy fits because their eight hundred words on county welfare have been edited down to seven hundred or some phrases have been changed or their piece appears "in the back of the magazine" or "below the fold" in a newspaper, when in actual fact they should be sobbing with joy that they managed to get into print at all. But big, shedding, slobbering dogs don't possess humility or irony or any sense of what we are pleased to call "reality."

Before you go nuts and indulge in behavior you've never seen in yourself before, try to remember this. Nobody (even if you're Norman Mailer—and you're *not*) in Africa cares. Nobody in Asia cares. Nobody in Lapland cares. Nobody in baseball cares, in golf, in soccer—except maybe if you're writing about baseball or golf or soccer. But even then they don't care about you: They care about baseball players and golfers, people who bang balls around.

Somebody somewhere may end up caring, but that's not

your business and to a large extent it's out of your hands. When your first work is published—that story, article, or poem—nobody is going to care except your immediate family, your circle of friends, and maybe your editor. What they really care about, what they're watching for, is whether or not you're going to turn into an asshole. Because the only people harder to be around than failed writers are pretentious jerks.

So there are a few things to do when you first get published and a few things not to do.

• **Remain Calm.** They always say that in elevators: Remain calm when the elevator gets stuck. They say it about earthquakes, too. Of course, the phrase itself is an admission that people don't stay calm in stuck elevators or when the living room furniture is shifting from the back wall over to the picture window. There's no way on earth to remain calm. But try to entertain the possibility of at least seeming calm.

When your work appears on a newsstand—*remain calm,* especially if you're in public. If you're home alone, you can shriek or jump up and down or punch your fist through the drywall or sit down and cry because it doesn't look the way you thought it would or they stuck a stupid headline on it or they misspelled your name; but don't do that in public. I think it's permissible to say to the man at the newsstand, "I *wrote* this! Isn't that amazing?" But don't get all involved in what he says back to you—he's working at a newsstand. *Remain calm.*

I'm assuming that your first work in print won't be a book but something in a magazine, newspaper, newsletter, or literary journal. Be sure to buy at least ten copies. (Don't have a tantrum if your publisher won't send you ten copies free!) Get ten copies, take them home, look at them for a while. Aren't they *great*?

Put five copies away in a drawer. They're part of the material you'll donate to a library after you get famous, part of the yellowed clippings your great-grandchildren will leaf through.

Then take the other five (or maybe a few more), find the perfect manila envelopes, and send them out to people in your personal and professional lives whom you respect and admire. Take some of your charming-note stationery and clip it on with a big paper clip: "I wanted you to have a copy of this! I hope you like it as much as I do." Already the shedding dog is growling: "Let them buy their own damn copies!" But they won't, because they're thinking about their own lives, and you'll just feel blue and put upon when you realize later that they not only didn't read your work, they didn't even notice when it came out.

• **Don't Be Vengeful!** You can send out copies to your most bitter enemies (in fact, it's a lot of fun to do that), but be sure to keep your notes as clear as consommé. Your note may say, in invisible ink, "I hope you're sorry now, you slut!" But the regular ink has to say: "I wanted you to have a copy of this. I hope you like it as much as I do. It reminds me of a better time, when we had so much fun." You have no control over what friends, enemies, or editors think. You just need to send out some copies of your work—with gracious, short, neutral notes.

Don't assume everyone has read whatever it is you've written. Nobody ever reads anything you've written! Again, they've got their own lives to live. If you want someone to read it, send him a copy.

• **Learn How to Say "Thank You" and "No Kidding!"** If someone sidles up to you and says, "I read that thing you wrote in the *Daily News* a while ago," you must on no account say, "What did you think?" Because you might get an answer you don't like. In fact, it's pretty certain you won't get an answer you'll like unless that someone says, "It's the greatest thing I've read since the New Testament!" (and even then you'll be thinking, "Matthew, Mark, Luke, John, those second-rate hacks! Does this person have no *taste?*") What you say is: *"No kidding!"* Which very adroitly bats the ball over into their court, and they almost always have to say, "I liked it." Or, "It was good. I was surprised!" Or, "Nice work." In which case you say, *"Thank you."* Or if they're mean or competitive enough to say "I don't know how you got started on such a loopy tangent," you give them a big, amiable grin and say, *"No kidding!"* When they say, "You know, my mother was horrified by what you wrote," you smile and say, *"No kidding!"*

That's *it*. You never want to ask, "What didn't she like about it?" Because it's none of your business.

• **Try Not to Bitch or Whine!** (How I wish I could follow my own advice on this one.) But give it your best shot. Don't weep or start fistfights or write irate letters because the editor has changed words on you. (The way to deal with this is "up front," as they say. Suggest to the editor, after he's accepted your work, "You're welcome to *cut* this as much as you want, but please don't change anything without running it by me first. Thank you!") Don't have a fit about placement, either, at the editor or for the benefit of your friends and enemies. When someone says, with an enigmatic leer, "I see you ended up on the last page," give them an equally enigmatic look and say, with deep significance, "*No kidding!*" And don't whine. No, "Oh, I hate that illustration. They utterly didn't get what I was doing." When somebody says to you, "What did you think of that illustration?" answer back: "What did *you* think?" In which case they'll have to say something that will allow you either to say "Thank you" or "No kidding!" And that's the end of it.

"How interesting!" is also a viable response, but not the best one, because it encourages people to go on, and you don't want them to go on. You want to skate through these initial encounters—in which your "self" as a writer is going public— as briefly and unthreateningly as possible. (I know there's a whole other school of thought on this, the idea that you turn into Norman Mailer and drink a lot and go to parties and pick fights. I admit that in the old days, I poured my share of drinks on people who didn't believe in my "work" and sent "irate" letters to editors and burst into tears over the phone, but such behavior is counterproductive, and I always had to apologize—because I'd been an idiot!)

Above all, don't get upset because your friends and family don't love your work enough. Because nobody could ever love your work enough. Have you heard the phrase "That kid's got a face only a mother could love"? Your work is your child; *you're* the one who has to love it, even though it may still be a little funny-looking.

———

Now that your first work is out, it's time to take a (covert, discreet) look at what might be the beginning of the rest of your career. How's your *mailing list*? This is the time to start working on it in earnest. Because there's going to be a book somewhere in your future, and that means book signings and parties and more mailing lists. It's separate from your address book, but you can start with that. You put some addresses into the computer and then you do that some more.

When you take a class at a community college, you should be the one to suggest exchanging addresses with your classmates. When you get a Christmas card from someone you know only faintly, save that address! When someone writes you a personal check for her share of the office gift, save that address. When the guy at the tire store or the car dealership or the framer's gives you a business card, save that address! When you serve on a committee at church or volunteer at the hospital or belong to a service group or send your kids to a private school, save those addresses.

A mailing list is a lifelong project: It's a way—another way—of connecting yourself to the literary world. It's a way that the "professional" separates himself or herself from victimized, failed writers, who do nothing when their book comes out, trying to make paralysis equate with "integrity," letting the book succeed on "merit alone."

And after your first publication, it's *really* time to start a bank account, money to be spent only on your writing. (I don't care if you're broke or poor; put in five dollars a week!) Every hundred dollars you save will be more useful than you can ever know when your first book comes out. And if you go twenty years without publishing your first book, you'll have enough money, God knows, for a very splashy Farewell to My Literary Dreams vacation.

So work on that mailing list.

Start that bank account.

And although you don't need an agent to place short pieces, now's the time to be thinking cagily about finding one. Five or ten years from now, you don't want to be the rumpled, pathetic person waving your arm in the air at a writers' conference, wailing—with great feeling—"How do I find an *agent*??!!" (Would you go out to a singles' bar and howl, "How do I find a *girlfriend*"? No!)

You want to lodge the word *agent* in the back of your mind.

Read the writers' interviews in *Publishers Weekly*. They always mention their agents. Start a computer file called "Agents." If you happen to go to any writers' conferences, be sure to choose the panel that features the agents. They're there partly to serve the community and partly in the romantic belief that there might be a writer out there, *the* writer that they've been put on earth to find.

Go up afterward, shake their hands, ask quietly for their business cards. Put that name in the computer under "Agents."

Then, when you take that first trip to New York, remember: *agents*. Write them some charming notes and ask for appointments. This is a lifelong plan, remember.

———

But wait a minute: Am I getting ahead of myself? Just how do you "send something out" in the first place?

Make a short list of periodicals where you'd like to see your work published. (Save *The New Yorker* for much later in your career!) Literary etiquette maintains that double or multiple submissions are out of the question. So send your piece out to one publication at a time.

Remember to double-space. Remember to spell-check. Then print it out and read it *carefully* for typos. Give it to a friend you can trust to look for the same thing. You don't want her value judgments; you just want information on repetitions and typos.

Be sure the best-quality paper is in your printer and that you're using the least obnoxious, least offensive font.

Your first page should look like this:

Joe Smith
1111 Black Street
Colorado Springs, CO 10704
(phone #)
(e-mail)

THE TIDES
by
Joe Smith

Your name and address should go in the upper-left-hand corner, and maybe your phone number and your e-mail address. Nothing else. No "copyright blah blah," no "10,221 words." Those are the marks of the rank amateur. The title comes in the middle of the page, all caps, then (double space) "by," then (double space) your name, then (two double spaces) your story or article begins. You'll only have room for four or five lines. Then "-1-" at the bottom.

Start again on the second page with the number in the upper-*right*-hand corner, along with your last name: "Smith-2."

Be sure to put numbers and your name on all the pages, since editors are disorganized. If they drop your manuscript, you want to be sure they can put it back together in the proper order without harming their brains.

Use your charming-note stationery for a cover letter. Make it short! It's not the story of your life. Just a paragraph on what the piece is about, a paragraph on who you are, and a last one about why you think the piece is right for that publication.

In this day and age, it's wise to include the material on disk as well.

You have two manila envelopes—one to send to the publication; the other, self-addressed, stamped, and folded neatly in two. I used to buy fancy commemorative stamps for the return envelope, figuring that whatever happened, I'd at least have a swell stamp collection, and I do.

After you mail something out, wait a month. After that, if you hear nothing, it's okay to write a follow-up note, saying you hope the manuscript got there safely or something of the sort. Be gracious. *Remain calm.* But by the same token, don't wait a year wringing your hands and waiting for them to decide whether they want something or not. Write them cheerful notes once a month.

When you see one of your own self-addressed envelopes in the mail, don't weep or put your fist through that wall. Open it up and *immediately* send a thank-you note—remember? Then slide your piece in another envelope and send it to the next publication on your list.

Keep doing that. And keep doing it. Finally, someone will accept the piece. That's when your friends, family, and enemies will scrutinize you closely to see if you're going to turn into a world-class jerk.

That's when you keep your shedding ego on a short leash, send out some copies to your friends and enemies, and practice saying "No kidding!" and "Thank you!" *Remain calm,* start a writing bank account, think quietly about an agent. And try as hard as you can to remain a decent human being.

PART II

The Writing

Chapter 10

Character

It might seem easy to write about "character." Haven't enough actors gone on and on about being in or out of "character"? Haven't we all had Henry James's words drummed into our heads: "What is character but action? What is action but character?" Haven't we, most of us, pondered the distinction that E. M. Forster made between "flat" and "round" characters? Don't we all have some kind of clue about "characterization"? But it's hard writing about it, like describing breathing or how to drive a car with a stick shift.

Character is so close to us and all around us that we sometimes have trouble seeing it. And although it sounds like heresy, I'm not at all sure that James or Forster were trying to make it easier for other people to write; they were just ruminating in a fairly highbrow and elitist way about what made *them* such good writers.

It might be fun trying to look at character another way (because, for one thing, James and Forster had lives of leisure, education, gentility, time for afternoon tea—made by somebody else—and endless hours for philosophy and theory). Until the rest of us get time to sit down for cucumber sandwiches, there are other ways to look at the characters who are going to be important in our lives and our work.

What if you quickly made a list of the ten most "important" people in your life? Without thinking about it, or trying to make a good impression on anyone, or a bad impression either? Whom do you love? Who betrayed you? Whom did you betray? Who drives you nuts? Who's out of your reach? Who's your role model? Who's your benchmark for insanity?

Quick! Write the list! That's what I'm going to do. I'm not going to try to get fancy about it:

1. My mother. She was beautiful and funny, and she never loved me. In fact, she couldn't stand me. Goddamnit!

2. My father. Handsome and funny and maybe a failed writer, maybe a successful one. He sometimes lived in poverty, but he was wealthy in words. Women loved him.

3. Billy See. How did *he* get on this list? A beautiful boy in the tenth grade at Marshall High. Small-boned and blue-eyed. I had such a crush on him. (No relation to the Richard See I finally married or the See name I kept.)

4. Judy Albaum. My best friend in graduate school. So smart we called her the "answer lady." Some of the best hours of my life were spent on the phone with Judy.

5. Lisa, my beautiful and accomplished older daughter. She had a tough childhood, and sometimes she seems aloof. But

I've never met a more tenderhearted person. Something in her has always reminded me of

6. Jackie, my best friend since the seventh grade. We walked home from school together. Jackie looked like a traditional sexpot even then, but she was—and is—virginal, unspoiled, aloof, childlike.

7. Clara, my beautiful, accomplished younger daughter, sturdy, fearless, heroic, headstrong, passionately committed to helping the human race. Insanely funny.

8. Dash Chandler, Clara's baby son. So beautiful it scares me.

Now wait just a *minute*! I've only got two more slots, and I've got two iffy ex-husbands and a wonderful man I lived with for twenty-seven years and I haven't included E. M. Forster or the women who invented birth control pills or the Virgin Mary or my other two wonderful grandsons. And what if I want to write science fiction and none of this pertains? Except, don't worry. It pertains.

I'm going to have to go with:

9. Tom Sturak, my second husband. Beautiful; he was beautiful. Very funny when he wanted to be. Short-tempered. Capable of being mean as a snake. (Or maybe I was just a pouting sore loser, a fountain of tears when he was around.)

10. Mrs. Wilheim, the mother of one of my junior high friends. The Wilheims were Hungarian, cultured, upper-middle-class. A balanced, sophisticated meal always came out of the Wilheim kitchen at 7 P.M. Mrs. Wilheim was the first human I ever heard who used the word *apocryphal* in conversation. Oh, and she was beautiful, mean, withholding, a trial to her daughter.

Quick, now, a short list of the other kind of "important" people you knew, and why. The ones who give you the willies. Who creep you out and you don't know why.

1. Tim Prewitt. He was a bad date and had crooked teeth. (My teeth were no picnic at that time, either.) He brought me a present and took me to the mountains. I hated him.

2. My stepfather. Poor drunk fool. He'd look at my mother and say, "If I were a gopher, I'd go for you." He liked canned string beans and Durkee dressing.

3. An ex-husband of my cousin's who got stuck with me at a dinner party and said, by way of conversation, "I hate niggers!"

4. A guy in his twenties I met on a Rhine cruise, with peach fuzz all over his head and a bad complexion, who said, in much the same vein, "I love missiles!"

5. A Persian man I went out in a rowboat with once.

6. A derivative poet I know with a bad haircut. He feels the same way about me. If not more so.

—

Isn't it a mystery, how we love some people, and hate others, and get hung up on ones who don't even know we exist? How we fall in love and stay in love and sometimes fall *out*? (I think of the couples who come to get their "relationships" fixed on *Oprah,* but sometimes you *see* the revulsion between those unfortunate pairs; it's as though they're sitting next to potato bugs. They can't stand each other. Sometimes it's because one of them has used the word *apocryphal* in conversation.)

—

I'm going to suggest that these ten—or sixteen—people on your list are your "characters" for life. There's a lot of post-modern literary theory going around that says there is no objective reality, that there are no genuine "characters" in the world and that there isn't even a real "self"—that the self is just a fictional construct we make up. Even though those post-modern critics give me the same weird feeling as that derivative poet, they may have a point.

We've only got our bodies, our brains, and our spirits. We only see what we can see. Life is refracted through our own eyes, ears, noses, mouths, skins. We have to make it up as we go along. I might like to have had Catherine the Great (who was reputed to have horses in derricks lowered over her to have sex with) on my list of my own ten most important people, because think of the scenes I could write! All that glitter and Russian lace! And torches—wouldn't the serfs have had torches? And think of that groaning derrick! And Catherine, all grim determination, with her legs wobbling around like a cockroach's antennae! And that poor horse.

But it didn't happen. God's present to me is my own life. It's not D. H. Lawrence's or Tolstoy's or Virginia Woolf's—much as I might like it to be. And, whoever is reading this, your life is your present, your dowry, your donnée. No one on earth is going to have the same list of Most Important Characters as you.

Before you respond that you're trying a life of art and literature to get *away* from your same old boring life, forget it. I was
down in Alabama once, on assignment, writing for a health
magazine, trying to get up the nerve to ask the wheelchair-
bound Governor Wallace whether or not he could still have sex,
and I hired a cab to take me to the home of Zelda, *the* Zelda,
who married Scott Fitzgerald, daughter of that mean old judge;
Zelda, temptress of the South, Daisy in *The Great Gatsby*.

The driver took me to a two-story house, on a street with a
lot of other two-story houses.

"This can't be it," I said. "The judge was very wealthy."

"This is it," he said. "People come here all the time." The
lawn hadn't been mowed.

So it must have been that Zelda's father was a moderately
big deal in a fairly small town, that's all. And when you look at
Zelda's photos, she seems astonishingly ordinary.

But if Fitzgerald made up a list of his ten most important
people (and Gatsby himself was an incorrigible list maker),
you know two of the people on Fitzgerald's list would be:

1. the judge, who said I didn't have enough money to
marry his daughter.
2. Zelda, the girl who said she loved me but went along
with her father until I got enough money to come back and
marry her. How *could* she?

As a writer, the importance of people is inside you. My
mother's rejection is the central event of my life. Enough people have said to me, "She was just a secretary," or, "She was

poor; she didn't know any better," or, "What does it matter what she thought anyway?" Or, "She was bipolar." Or, "She was depressive." Or, "She was mistaken." But it matters to me.

———

If the pope were to make a list of his ten most important people, you can bet that list would include the Virgin Mary, even though a large part of the world is not at all sure the Virgin Mary existed. And some of William F. Buckley's most beautiful and measured writing has been about the Virgin. She's part of his world; she's made his list.

The people in your life don't have to take a bodily form. They can be the great-grandfather who squandered the family fortune or ran off with a Gypsy. The father you never knew. The girl you haven't met yet. Or Mr. Right.

You don't want to fudge on this, though. You don't want to say:

1. Thomas Jefferson, because he made the world safe for Democracy.
2. Franklin Delano Roosevelt, because he brought our great country out of the Depression.

(But if you've seen *Jaws* 127 times, you might want to jot down Robert Shaw, as Quint, or that shark.)

———

Your characters are the ones you know something about. You may even have said to them, in a quarrel, "I know you better than you know yourself!" Whether, in fact, you do know them is open to debate. But they give you—in a form of cosmic refraction—unique access to your own soul and vision of life.

Doesn't *that* sound pretentious! But to be specific, if it hadn't been for Tom Sturak, number 9 on my list, I would never have known what it was like to be so consumed with anger that I could slug someone, and in fact, several times, I *did* slug him.

If it hadn't been for Mrs. Wilheim, number 10 on my list, I might have missed the whole world of intellectual aspiration that led me to getting my Ph.D.

If it hadn't been for number 4, Judy Albaum, I would have followed the conventions of my day and thought that men, by definition, were more interesting and powerful than women.

So by refraction, these characters illumine *my* character, shine lights into the dark cavern of *my* "self."

———

For instance, on Philip Roth's ten-most-important list, number 1 would probably have to be:

1. *my dick!*

But think about how brave and consistent Philip Roth has been in his life, going along with that truth, how that refraction has served him. In fictional terms:

2. the girl in *When She Was Good,* because she didn't get the absolute truth and importance of circumstances surrounding *my dick*!

3. Drenka in *Sabbath's Theater,* because she absolutely got the truth and importance of circumstances surrounding *my dick*!

You're not going to get any prose about the Virgin Mary from Philip Roth, and not just because he's Jewish.

But what a swell world it is that can include and embrace and make art from both the Blessed Mother and that fleshy appendage poking out of Philip Roth.

—

Look at your list. Pick a number. Cast that person up in front of your eyes, as Aristotle says. What's he like? *Don't* say, "Oh, five-foot-eleven, about 180 pounds." What does he *look* like? Zoom close to his skin, the way his flesh hangs on his skeleton, the way he stands or sits or lies. Where he puts his hands. How he breathes. Whether or not he's had a shower today. What he's wearing and why. What's his natural expression? Check out his eyes, the droop of his mouth, the tightness or looseness of his cheeks.

Henry James said, "What is character without action?" Your character doesn't have to jump off a building, but what does he do when he's moving? Where is he? What's he doing? *Cast him up in front of your eyes.* He's yours now. You own him. And from now on, it's a combination of what he does and what you want him to do that's going to make this character come alive.

—

Every once in a while, a reader perusing a book gets so excited by the truth of what he or she is reading that she (or he) has to stand up and take a few breaths, because the freaky beauty of it is like a hit to the solar plexus. It's happened to me four times that I remember:

Jack Kerouac writing about Dean Moriarty parking cars in Manhattan, before the real action of *On the Road* begins. I was in the L.A. public library and I had to get up.

Somewhere in the middle of *The Charterhouse of Parma*, I had to take a walk around the house, during a battle scene. I hadn't expected to. I was getting ready for qualifying exams in graduate school. I'd thought I was having a pretty miserable time reading, but Stendhal got me up off my chair.

Jayne Anne Phillips, putting a man through his paces, washing the family car in *Machine Dreams*.

Amy Tan in pages 20–30 of *The Joy Luck Club*, letting eight people live out one night in a Chinese-American home. The memory of my first marriage came back to me so hard that I thought I'd stop breathing.

—

You have your characters. You want to get at the *truth*, the truth beyond the truth. But don't try too hard. You see your character now and you've written some of him down. *Cast him up in front of your eyes*. What's he doing?

An old guy who's not on my list recently died. He was a professor when I was in graduate school, an interesting man in many ways, but not a person you'd ever call "nice." At the funeral, a pious young minister asked us to recall an image from the professor's life and then meditate upon it, to "commend Ronald into heaven." I closed my eyes and all I could remember was that Ronald had had this terrific crush on a student thirty years younger and one foot taller than he. The only image I could see was me sitting with them on a circular banquette in a very dark restaurant. I was on one side, the girl on the other, Ronald in the middle, but by the time the main course came, he'd pushed so far up against her that her left foot was anchored way out in the aisle so she wouldn't fall out of the booth.

Instead of meditating, I had to actively pray: Please, God, if there is a God, don't let this silly incident interfere in any way from letting Ronald into heaven, if there is a heaven.

You know what your characters are doing. Let them do it. Let them shoot a gun, wash a car, watch while the old friends set up the mah-jongg game.

You have an infinity of scenes to choose from. You're God in your universe; you get to choose. I remember my mother in gambling casinos playing the nickel slots. Or drunk as a lord, inexplicably snapping bedsheets in the middle of the night. Or laughing with her sister, playing "Kitten on the Keys" or "Nola." I can write about that. And have.

I also remember her making a wonderful sponge cake and covering it with homemade butter-cream frosting on a summer afternoon. Or crying—only once!—at dusk on the bed she shared with my dad, missing her own dead mother, she said. Or walking to the streetcar, excited to be on jury duty. I have trouble with these sweet images, since, as I've said, she couldn't stand me. But they're there in the bank. I can use them when I need to.

—

Now that you've got your character moving, open his mouth and let him talk. This can seem hard. Again, I've had students tell me, in the most piteous way, "I don't *do* dialogue," as though dialogue were murder or ironing or windows.

But the nice thing is: *You* don't have to "do" the dialogue. Your characters do it. They've been talking a blue streak all along. Close your eyes and listen. What do they say?

My number 3, Billy See, never said anything to me. He hung his head and blushed.

My number 8, my grandson Dash, says—at nineteen months—"Tuin it!" (for turn it). "Tuin it!"

My number 9, Tom Sturak, loved to begin his sentences to me with "The trouble with *you* is . . ."

"Jewish mah-jongg," says the dead mother in *The Joy Luck Club*. "They watch only for their one tile, play only with their own eyes."

Don't get haughty about it! You're not *making up* dialogue for Catherine the Great! "Attention, serflings! You may now lower the horse!"

All you have to do is listen.

Here's a warning. If you *don't* listen, if you go around arrogantly making up dialogue for your characters, all of them will sound like you, and that's one of the ways bad short stories and novels are written. (Also bad journalism, oddly enough. Because certain arrogant journalists make up their own quotes.)

Try to give up your "self." Put yourself on the back burner. Go to restaurants and listen. Can you hear the conversations around you? Do you catch the tune? Or, listen to a person who drives you nuts: "And don't you think that we might have a little kiss goodnight?"

Just . . . listen.

—

Many times, in creative writing courses, even though I earnestly give my students the same kind of information that I'm putting down here, I'll find myself hearing a story about a priest having sex in a confessional (without regard for those walls that separate priest from supplicant), a story where everyone has emerald eyes and the lead character is a noted brain surgeon or a landlady falls in love with "a mysterious Gypsy." The eyes of the other students glaze over; a torpor settles upon the room.

After a few open-ended, polite questions, someone's bound to ask, "Where'd you get the idea for the priest/brain surgeon/Gypsy?"

The student will answer defiantly, "I made it up. It's fiction."

"Well, but let me just ask you this: How does the priest manage to make love to the adulteress in the confessional? I'm not saying it can't be done, but how does he do it, since there's that wall between them? And why is that brain surgeon home with his wife at eleven in the morning? Don't surgeons usually operate early and then make their rounds before lunch? And how does that landlady know the stranger who's going to rent her furnished room is a Gypsy? How does she know he's not Guatemalan or Mexican or something else we have around here?"

And then, another round of questions: "Did you ever know any priests/brain surgeons/Gypsies?"

Of course, *no!* They don't have the beginning of a clue about any of those people. So then their classmates reiterate gently that it's generally a good idea to "write about what you know," and by then the person who wrote the story has stopped being defiant; he nods politely but exudes relief. Because it's over. He's taken his turn reading and his classmates didn't care for the story, but what does it matter? The story has nothing to do with *him*! Nobody is going to nail him for being a "bad" writer, because he really didn't write anything that would give anyone the opportunity to find out.

Then the conversation shifts into "Do you really have to murder someone in order to write about murder?" Or, "How can you write about boring people without being really boring?" Or, "You know, you can write about sex in a confessional if you want, but you really need to look at the inside of a confessional first." Or, "You might want to eyeball a real Gypsy before writing about one." And a mantle of precarious but bogus safety falls over the class: They may have all been absolutely bored to death, but nobody really had to risk anything.

Nothing has happened at all.

The real rule, at some level, looks to be *Don't* write what you know; write about what you *care* about. Not a priest you never met, but the one who got an unseemly hard-on when he danced with you at a sixth-grade formal at St. Francis of Assisi Elementary School. Or the brain surgeon who called you up on December 25 and said, "Merry Christmas! The cancer's gone up to your father's brain!" And, personally, I never met any real Gypsies, but I saw a caravan of them once, at the far end of a campground in the south of France: It looked very silvery and prosperous, but I wouldn't dare to put a Gypsy into any narrative of mine, because I don't know a thing about them.

You want to write about people you care about. You can dress them up any way you see fit. You can slam them together in composites or put knee breeches on them and let them fight in the Revolutionary War, but your characters ought to be some of the ten most important people in your life, or the six most creepy, or you'll bore the socks off your readers, and yourself as well.

—

A word about villains. You want to know your villains very well indeed or you're better advised not to go inside their heads at all.

A villain, by definition, is somebody different from "us." A villain is indecent, incomprehensible, from the land of "them." Who knows what makes them act the way they do? A decent human being can't figure them out! And part of our ongoing fiction about ourselves is that we're the good guys. The enduring paradox is that they think *they're* the good guys.

Cops think gang members are a little on the subhuman side. Gang members think cops are a little on the subhuman side. Years ago, soldiers going to the Korean War had to watch an educational film with cinematic tough guy William Bendix exhorting the troops to go out and "smash them Japs!" This was bewildering, because we'd already won *that* war. "Japs" had turned from villains back into regular people, but nobody had any anti-Korean films ready yet.

I'll never understand the man on my list who said "I hate niggers." Or the one who said "I love missiles," either.

You want to be careful about going into the head of someone you can't figure out. It's smarter to look at her carefully from the *outside*. I guess the classic example is Margot in Hemingway's "The Short Happy Life of Francis Macomber." For people who weren't made to read this in an English class, the story concerns four characters out in the African veld. Wilson, a brave white hunter, has contracted to take a client, Francis Macomber, and his wife, Margot, out on safari so that Francis can shoot a lion. The white hunter and his client's wife instantly start an affair. We're given to understand that this is okay because Francis is not a very manly man—his name is Francis, not Frank—and certainly Wilson is under no moral imperative. But what about Margot? Margot is hateful as a scorpion; she says one terrible thing after another . . .

But Francis is a coward! We know it before the lion hunt and during and after, when he gets off a bad shot, wounds the lion, and is more than willing to just walk off, leaving the lion perhaps to harm some innocent passerby and to suffer greatly. The fourth character here is the wounded lion, who doesn't feel very well.

It's become fashionable for many critics to make fun of Hemingway for his weird ideas about the manly code and so on. But he was a writer—especially in his short stories—both meticulous and brave. He doesn't hesitate to go into Wilson's mind (if Hemingway doesn't know about what it is to be a fearless white hunter, who does?). He also goes unflinchingly into Francis Macomber's mind, because he has a fairly flawless idea of what it is to be unmanned by physical fear. And in a stunning tour de force he goes into the lion's mind, after the animal is wounded. But Hemingway draws the line with Margot, because only God knows what's going on in that creepy little head of hers. Hemingway can't, and won't, go into her mind to find out.

Look at the list of your ten most important people and your list of people who creep you out. Your villains are lurking somewhere in there. You may know *how* they act but not *why*; and that's good.

Cosmically speaking, maybe God himself is as baffled by the mystery of evil as we are. Maybe villains are only among us to thicken the plot, to give all of "us" something to do.

Chapter 11

Plot

Your characters have got to have something to do. That's "plot." I think men and women have very different feelings for plot, and traditionally, men enjoy the advantage.

The Iliad and *The Odyssey*, for instance, are long, male action-adventures with clear-cut beginnings, middles, ends. Every basketball, football, and baseball game is an event with a beginning, a middle, and an end, victory and defeat ensured. Men have been building bridges and buildings, and destroying bridges and buildings, and raping and pillaging women and children, or stoutly defending women and children, since the beginning of time.

They've been trained to do all that stuff and then they've been trained to talk about it. Men are raised to have enough self-esteem to take it for granted that whatever they do is interesting. Women have been trained to listen. Have you ever heard a garage band playing and you go take a peek and there are five or six girls just wailing away while their boyfriends sit politely waiting for them to finish? No. Because it would never happen.

Plot implies that not only does art have a beginning, a middle, and an end but that life does, too. And that's more or less true. We're born, we live, we die: beginning, middle, and end. But plot is not very good at addressing the endless hours when you're taking care of a sick kid or the couple of hours you can spend talking on the phone with a friend and at the end you can't remember all that you've said, but you feel better. Plot thrives on event; it thrives on conflict, even though most of us go through our days routinely, contentedly, and, generally speaking, without much conflict at all.

From a man's point of view, all the stories may already have been told. Men have certainly been at it long enough. Maybe all the explorers have already left home and discovered the world and come back. Maybe all the bridges and buildings have been constructed. Maybe all wars look alike.

Feminist critics complain that women, through history, have been stuck with all the wife/mother/lover plots. In fiction, it does tend to be true: Women get stuck being the wife, the mom, the lover—even in novels written by women.

In the twentieth century, it was fashionable for a while for men to sell plot short in relation to character. Character-driven literature was seen as superior to plot-driven narrative. That may only have been because the male literary elite attempted nothing more strenuous than lifting martinis to their lips and jumping their friends' wives. (I think, particularly, of John Updike.) But all along, other men, who saw life differently, were writing excellent novels based mostly on plot.

—

I just did what I told myself I would never do during this proj-ect. I checked out Anne Lamott's marvelous book about writ-ing, *Bird by Bird,* to see what she writes about plot, and she says what I thought I remembered her saying: "Don't worry about plot. Worry about the characters. . . . All you can give us is what life is about from your point of view. You are not going to be able to give us the plans to the submarine. Life is not a submarine. There are no plans." Yes, that's certainly true, ex-cept for the men who build submarines and go to sea in them. Life *is* a submarine to them. Coal is life to coal miners; trucks are life to truckers—and truck stops, to their waitresses; bank robbers must think that life is one big heist.

I agree with Anne that all you can give us is life from your point of view. But you can take a leap of the imagination every once in a while.

And plot, more than any other aspect of writing, provides pleasure and hypnosis. The reader needs to find out what hap-pens next, even if he's read it before and already knows. Melville is fine, he's perfectly swell, but you don't stay up all night reading *Moby-Dick* because you can't help yourself.

Professors are always exhorting you to read great books to expand your imagination, "broaden your horizons," and re-fine your style. Great books contain the templates to "great book" plots, but I've found that where I really learn about plot is by reading guy-written, plot-driven novels that don't pretend to be masterpieces. They hold the reader's attention simply by the delicious surprise of what happens next: C. S. Forester's

Horatio Hornblower series. Any book by Elmore Leonard. Any book by Carl Hiaasen.

Horatio Hornblower enters His Majesty's Royal Navy sometime in the late eighteenth century as a lowly midshipman, fights all over the world for king and country, and especially through those Napoleonic Wars. His is a world of tall ships and holystoned decks and a Central American madman named El Supremo and a series of women, coming in every size, station, and social class, who love Hornblower more than life itself. Hornblower is a hero, but he is plagued by every kind of psychological doubt: a "modern man" wandering through life in silk knee breeches, worried sick—for at least the first few books in the series—that the buckles on his shoes are only pinchbeck and he can't afford gold. The ongoing centerpieces of these novels are old-fashioned naval battles, with masts splintering and sails shredding and seamen whose names you didn't catch being blown to pink foam by cannon fire, and smoke everywhere and blood running in the scuppers.

Any book by Elmore Leonard is chocolate cake for me. He creates a world of jailbirds and con men and drug runners and undertakers. People live in rough, unrefined places like Detroit or Daytona Beach. They're always killing each other at random or by mistake or on purpose. No one has to go through the indignity of holding a steady job, except for cops, and you can't call what they do work. Leonard's landscape is crawling with corrupt politicians and stolen money and nasty cadavers; his books are chock-full of information about pop music, harvesting cucumbers, embalming stiffs. The man's a genius or a maniac. He has said that he lives a simple life, but he could live to be a hundred and never run out of gore, wit, characters: *plot*.

Carl Hiaasen is a journalist at *The Miami Herald*. He hates developers and what they've done to the Florida wilderness. He tends to write books with antiheroes—newspapermen and P.R. flunkies. His idea of a story in *Native Tongue* is: What if sleazy gangsters opened up a yucky theme park called the Amazing Kingdom of Thrills and in order to get government grant money they dipped a couple of house rats into India ink to create a new endangered species called blue-tongued mango voles? The rats get lost and somebody has to get murdered, but it's cunningly managed so that the (unwitting) murderer is a surly rogue killer whale who hates the color kelly green. The victim is found wearing a kelly-green sport shirt, having left behind a bogus suicide note: I SORRY BUT I CAN'T GO ON. NOW THAT MY WORK IS OVER, SO AM I. There's also another killing by a baboon, and a weight lifter on steroids, who chews off his own foot. To my mind, Hiaasen's scenes are separate, perfect jewels. He's a radiant reminder that literature can head in eleven directions at once.

This kind of novel is generally (but not always) written by men. But what about all those hundreds and hundreds of years lived *inside* houses, the lives of women with "a bit of sewing in their laps," as Virginia Woolf argued valiantly at the beginning of the last century. She was talking about wife/mother/lover plots. And although I'm going to mention three women writers who are terrific at plot, creating highly structured stories that stand alone, it's good to remember that the great preponderance of fiction written by women still has to do with being treated badly by men or getting rescued by a man or running off with a man or snagging a man or being driven crazy by parents or having children and loving them more than life itself.

There's absolutely nothing wrong with constructing wife/mother/lover plots, where women are the main focus, the center of attention. (Male readers may be a little less than anxious to read your book, but so what?) Mary McCarthy built *A Charmed Life* around a young wife telling lies about a dinner party. Sue Miller's *The Good Mother* has page after page of lovely conversation between a mother and her child; then an awful man comes and takes her child away. In Virginia Woolf's *The Waves*, I'm not sure *what* happens. Women think and feel. The "plans for the submarine" don't enter into any of this, only the recipe for pot-de-crème.

All my life I've attempted to construct traditional plots. But instead of a beginning/middle/end, I almost always end up with: chat chat chat chat chat/sex/chat chat chat chat chat chat/disaster/chat chat chat chat chat/"lyrical" reconciliation. That's the best I can do. It's like Anne Lamott says: I don't have the plans to the submarine.

But here are three women who've constructed novels with wonderful plots. One of them, Isabel Allende, had her plot handed to her: The Chilean government was illegally overthrown; her uncle was head of the government. Rather than focusing on the "historical" part of this tragedy, the "*his* story," of what happened, in *The House of the Spirits* Allende chose to focus on the tale of one particular family. She hooks up the inside and the outside lives of those Chileans, so by the time the government does fall and innocent people are rounded up to die in the municipal stadium of the capital, we mourn them all as if we're related to them, because we've seen them, as family, over the years. We've seen the grandma in the corner of the living room get older and older until she dies and nobody notices; we've heard the stirring speech of one of the women of the household about how doing good works does no good at all but we must go on doing them anyway. Allende takes history and reveals it to us through the women's lenses.

The next book is hard to find, but so is gold ore. Rose Tremain's *The Way I Found Her* is a masterpiece. (Don't you just love how men still own the language—*his*tory? *master*-piece?) It's one of a kind, and after you've read it, you can't forget it. Lewis, a thirteen-year-old boy from Devon, in England, accompanies his very beautiful mother, a translator, to Paris, where they stay in the lavish apartment of the beautiful millionaire-romance-novelist Valentina Gavrilovich, who introduces him to an entirely different world.

Valentina has come from poverty-stricken Russia and makes up for it now with silks, satins, marvelous foods, and a string of lovers. She's plump and forty, but Lewis develops a huge crush on her. He's bedeviled by sexual longings, but he's still a kid! He plays with an action figure named Elroy, and tags around unnoticed by the grown-ups, befriending a roofer named Didier and a gentleman neighbor with dyed-tangerine hair . . .

Lewis's mother turns out to be a heartless snake. Then, about halfway through the book, Valentina is kidnapped. Lewis is the only one who cares, the only one who can find her. The little boy is precocious, a language and computer whiz. He's reading two books at once, Alain-Fournier's *Le Grand Meaulnes* as well as *Crime and Punishment*. Those two novels, plus a comprehensive knowledge of Parisian roof tiles, tie the narrative up into an exquisitely complex package. There's real murder here, heartbreaking death, screened through a world that at first looks as if it's only made up of women, children, and a servant or two.

Why haven't you heard of this book? Because it's unique, I suspect. I can't think of anything else like it in the English language. But I believe only a woman could have written it with such tenderness, taking a naïve boy child and turning him into a young man doomed by fate, the best part of his life well behind him by the time he's fifteen.

To shake free of traditional wife/mother/lover plots, a woman must be willing to step into a larger world (if she can, or wants to). One of my favorite novels is Annie Proulx's *The Shipping News*. (About the time that I'm writing this, the movie came out. Stay away from it. It's a disgrace.) Proulx's hero, the wretched Quoyle, is no movie star. He's ugly, pimpled, desperate, and ignorant, and he's been left in a sterotypically "female" position: dumped by a heartless spouse, who then dies in a fiery car crash. His dour aunt appears and suggests that there's only one thing for him to do—pack up his kids and his aunt and go back where they all came from, Newfoundland.

"And search ye all the world around from Zanzibar to Flanders, yet ne'er can find the equal of the all-round Newfoundlander." I know that verse because I once lived there. Newfoundland is the "submarine" in this case, and Quoyle's task is to find out how to live there. He finds true love—predictably—but the other thing he does is teach himself how to write, how to put together newspaper stories, invent headlines, make his mark in this strange, primitive, utterly out to lunch world, where hotel doorknobs come off in your hand, locking you in snowbound rooms; where the blue-plate special is apt to be fried salami; where snow and strong drink and craziness are everything. The plot itself springs from the weirdness of the land and the language. And although it's about a man, a man would probably never write it, because its "hero" is so unattractive, pathetic, and abandoned to begin with.

—

Despite their differences, men and women face oddly parallel problems when they deal with plot: Men's stories have been written to death, and women are still figuring out how to write about their experience. But plots—like those elusive plans for the submarine—are made to be used again and again. You don't build just one submarine and throw the plans out! More humbly, plots are like wooden hangers in a closet. You don't refuse to hang up your shirt because that hanger's already been used a few times.

I'm looking now at a current list of books from *The Washington Post* that I've been assigned to review:

My Happy Life, by Lydia Millet. A girl child is beaten, raped, abandoned, placed in an asylum, and abandoned again. She's happy, though.

Limbo, and Other Places I Have Lived, by Lily Tuck. Short stories in which a series of intelligent, sensitive women are mistreated, betrayed, and abandoned by a series of loutish men.

Tepper Isn't Going Out, by Calvin Trillin. An elderly man in New York City refuses to move his parked car.

More, Now, Again, by Elizabeth Wurtzel. A nonfiction account of a young woman's drug addiction and recovery, during which she is mistreated and abandoned by an unsuitable man.

Leaving Katya, by Paul Greenberg. A young man, in love with all things Russian, marries a Russian girl, who gives him no end of trouble.

Whitegirl, by Kate Manning. A white girl marries a beautiful but hot-tempered black celebrity. No good comes of it.

Violence, Nudity, Adult Content, by Vince Passaro. A really awful guy is unexpectedly kicked out by his wife. Against a background of extreme perversion and crime, he must find a way to redeem himself.

Savannah Blues, by Mary Kay Andrews. A single woman, dumped by her lout husband, finds a way to make a living dealing in antiques and picks up a new boyfriend on the way.

In the Forest, by Edna O'Brien. A boy child in an Irish village suffers his mother's death and is placed in a series of institutions. Years later, he returns to murder three villagers. Who's at fault?

—

There's nothing fancy about any of these plots. You can see how repetitive (and useful) they are. You don't have to be a plot *genius* like Elmore Leonard or Rose Tremain. You don't have to build a state-of-the-art submarine. A sturdy rowboat, even a wooden coat hanger, will do just fine.

Chapter 12

Point of View

You know those group photographs with at least a couple of rows of people where someone in the first row is taking it all seriously and some person behind him or her is holding up two fingers, making the serious person look silly? Or where a TV news reporter unlucky enough to be out on assignment in some bad neighborhood is standing there trying to be dignified while a flock of street urchins are waving their arms behind him, sabotaging the whole enterprise?

Or recall, if you're a woman, sitting by a friend who's crying her eyes out because her boyfriend has been cheating on her—notoriously—and she, of course, is the very last to know. You feel sorry for her and say the right things, but you've seen that guy with his new girlfriend out behind the elementary school, down at the gas station, and over at Long's Drugs (in the sexual-aids section). How could she not have *seen* it?

Remember listening to "pundits" from both political parties on TV as they blat out their opposing views and, sure, they're doing it to make a living, and they probably all go out to dinner afterward together, but sometimes they're so convincing and so downright unexpected in their points of view that you take it in, sincerely startled. Wait a minute! You're saying Augusto Pinochet was a *hero of the people*? Was there something I missed here? Didn't he massacre thousands of dissidents down there in Chile? But we're always missing something. Most of us have missed World War I, and we've all missed the Spanish-influenza epidemic and the black plague seven hundred years ago and what happened to our parents before we were born and to our lovers before we met them. And when our kids walk off to school every day, that's *it*—we can't follow them. Thus, the question "How was school today?" and the reply "Fine."

Our points of view, literal and figurative, define us as much in life as which gene pool we've climbed out of. If we are poor, we won't get to *experience* the homes of the rich, or fashion shows or yacht races or country club dinners or the first-class section of airplanes. If we are born rich, we drive through middle-class neighborhoods—miles and miles of them—without the remotest clue about what's going on behind those walls. If we are Americans, we can be taken on tours of the Amazon jungle where we stand around watching "natives" sullenly making mush out of roots, but we have no idea what those people may be thinking, and vice versa. (Weren't Americans genuinely surprised on September 11, 2001, when it turned out at least half the world hated us?)

In writing, point of view shapes everything we do and gives it a structure, if we pay attention. Sins against point of view create problems that make us look like numskulls.

—

Point of view, in the English language, has always been divided into four categories: first person, third person, limited omniscient, and omniscient. Then, during the early part of the twentieth century, Virginia Woolf and James Joyce invented "stream of consciousness"—that is, the way minds actually "work."

First person: the prose that begins "Call me Ishmael" or "I am an American, Chicago-born." It's just "I" talking, Philip Marlowe discovering the clues.

"I got up and went to the window. The streets were icy, and a thick shroud of fog obscured the village. How appropriate, I thought, that the spires and towers had faded into nothing. I hurried back to the fire, where cook had laid out an appetizing tea."

The "I" is an "eye," a camera, pointing in one direction out of the eyes of the first, and most important, person. (Think of Christopher Isherwood writing "I am a camera with its shutter open, quite passive . . .")

Many a picky critic has dissed the first person as being the last refuge of morons: You're limited by what you can "see" writing from the first person. But what they may really mean is that it's much harder to make terrible mistakes.

I looked at George. He was glad to see me.

Your editor will tell you—and probably make you mad by doing so—that it has to be:

I looked at George. He *seemed* glad to see me.

Why? Because you (or that *first person*, that "I") can't *know* what George is thinking!

Third person:

Phil looked at George. George looked back.

Okay, here's limited omniscient:

Phil looked over at George. His old poker buddy seemed glad to see him. Phil couldn't have cared less.

The point of view is third person (because we're using *he* or *she*), but it only goes into Phil's mind. That's the "limited" part. Here's "omniscient," where the author knows everything about everybody. (And I expect that people who already know this will be sighing with exasperation, but the people who don't know yet, don't know, so now's their time to learn):

Phil looked at George.

George has aged considerably, Phil thought. I wonder if he knows I've been bonking his wife.

George returned Phil's gaze with a level stare. If only you knew the favor you've done me, he mused. Now I can run off with Octavio. We can go to Finland together and take a lot of saunas.

(In other words, the author knows *everything* going on in all his characters' minds.)

Here's a stab at stream of consciousness. I admit it's not my strong suit.

Finland, snow, smell of birch and eucalyptus and semen. Pink flesh yielding, steam, smoke, sweat, all inwardly, downwardly, now!

Luckily, from my point of view, at least, stream of consciousness is going out of style—not because writers don't love to play with it, but because readers generally find it pretentious and lose interest pretty quickly. (What if you "reinvented the language," as James Joyce claimed to do, but after forty years or so your readers just began to drift politely away?)

Beginning writers love to use the omniscient point of view, because they think they know everything about the story they're writing; and in one way they do. After all, they're the ones who thought up their stories. But it's harder than you think to know what's going on in everybody's head.

I had a rough lesson in point of view about ten years ago, when I went with my little brother, then about twenty-three, to watch him pitch a movie script at USC film school, along with about two dozen hotshot would-be auteurs. The department only had funds to make three films, so there was a lot of competition.

Young men were there from all over the world—no women that I noticed—and each had ten minutes to pitch their stories. A Turkish guy had an idea: A young Turkish artist dedicates his life to his art; a young prostitute willingly throws herself under a streetcar, leaving him an inheritance so that he can go on with his work. A rough-looking Chicano guy wrote a nice treatment about a rough-looking Chicano guy whose girlfriend is squashed by a truck, leaving him the freedom to go on with his work. A young Chinese guy wrote about a Chinese novelist who was harassed during the Cultural Revolution and whose girlfriend, after a stirring monologue about the transcendence of art, gives herself sexually to a bureaucrat so that the novelist can go on with his work. I was there because my brother had adapted one of my short stories about our dad stealing some doughnuts during the Great Depression. My brother had changed this to a story about a young journalist down in El Paso whose girlfriend is killed in a shoot-out, which, due to circumstances I can't remember right now, enables him to go on with his work.

They *wish*!

Can you see the point-of-view problems here? If you were able to interview all those fictional prostitutes and girlfriends and ask *them* just why is it that they are so willing to give up their lives for these guys and their promising careers, they wouldn't have much to say. "Because the author wants me to. Now excuse me. I've got to fall off this balcony."

You can infer, from the "treatments" of these screenwriters, that they want success in their careers and that they wouldn't mind if *someone else* died for it. They would dearly love to have some passion and hot sex in their lives, but they'd just as soon have those women (embarrassing fantasies that they are) drop out of sight before their fannies spread.

Those screenwriters knew next to nothing about young women. That didn't stop them from writing about them, though. That's one of the problems with the omniscient point of view.

What if you looked at your stories as classified information?

That means you only go into your characters' minds on a need-to-know basis. If they *absolutely* need to think or feel something, you can let them do it; otherwise, let them alone. Don't make a damn fool of yourself if you don't need to.

Here are three short examples.

Unless you went to graduate school, you probably never got to read the old Icelandic sagas. They're great—really! Full of blood and strange conversations. They all have to do with the Icelandic Smiths going on over, in a big family group, to spend the afternoon with the Icelandic Joneses. The ladies at the Jones house, fixing lunch, get worried.

"You know what happened the last time we all got together?"

"Sure I know. We lost forty-eight cousins and twelve uncles at that last picnic, but there's no telling *them* anything."

"You're right! They don't ask us, do they?"

Then the Icelandic Jones boys and the Icelandic Smith boys start playing handball against the side of the house and somebody accuses somebody else of cheating and the next thing you know, all the men have pulled out their ice axes and are busily engaged in hacking one another to death, while inside the kitchen the women exchange gloomy remarks:

"I knew this was going to happen."

"It always happens when the Smiths come over."

"There'll be fewer mouths to feed tonight."

There's an *extremely limited point of view* in these sagas. You never know more than what a fairly smart neighbor walking around outside those houses might know. There are no forays into Icelandic bedrooms (perish the thought!) and certainly none into the minds of those truculent men (who are out on the ice floes by now, turning the whole river red with blood) or into the minds of the women (who are conveniently located right by the windows, where they can look outside, watch the carnage, and comment about it). It makes for an extraordinary, fact-based narrative, a that's-the-way-it-is attitude, which you can also see, more recently, in Dashiell Hammett's hard-boiled novels, where, for instance, you don't have a clue what Sam Spade or any of the shady characters he deals with are thinking. You can watch them blush or flush or hit each other or even (somewhat chastely) make love, or watch their eyes gleam "yellowly," but their thoughts are off-limits to the reader and the writer, because, to be perfectly frank, who of us has a real clue about what anybody else is thinking? It's hard enough to keep up with what *we're* thinking at any given moment.

Hemingway, remember, didn't go into the minds of women. He always took care to see them from the outside. "Oh, darling, I've been so miserable," Brett says to Jake Barnes early in *The Sun Also Rises*. But we're going to have to take Brett's word for it, as filtered through Jake's perceptions. Even in the Hemingway-drivel from *For Whom the Bell Tolls*, when the love-besotted young Spanish peasant girl—aptly named Rabbit for her propensity to breed—experiences what we're to understand is her first orgasm and asks Robert Jordan, "Did the earth move for you?" she's only asking, and he's only hearing. The author would never dream of going inside her mind, which shows, I think, that Hemingway was a smart enough writer to *stay away from what he didn't know.*

Not to say that we all have to stay out of the minds of characters of the opposite sex—just that we need to think carefully about which minds we're barging into.

None of us should believe everything we hear. A man who *tells* a woman he'll call her isn't necessarily going to do it. He's just talking. And women lie to men. Who ever heard of a woman who has said, just after sex, "You're about the same as everybody else." (Although I did hear of a lady once who remarked, "Well! That counts as the second-best time in my life!")

Because I have some good manners and lots of civility myself, I won't mention by name the many dunderheaded male followers of Hemingway who go tromping into their female characters' minds and genitals, endowing them with orgasms that go on for page after purple page.

Another kind of example: By a fluke, and the generosity of friends, my good friend Jackie Joseph and I got an assignment to write one of the very dumbest episodes of the old TV series *Barnaby Jones*. It had an autistic child in it who couldn't talk, but that presented no problems for us, because she didn't have to talk! On the other hand, my warmhearted friend shot down every possible murder scenario: "I just don't see why anybody would want to kill each other over this," she'd say. "Why don't they just sit down and talk things over?"

Except that there had to be a murder at the bottom of page 8, along with four suspects, otherwise Barnaby would never get to come on the case and we'd never get paid. Finally, we thought up an unfaithful husband. We could see how several people—his wife, his boss, his girlfriends—might want to kill him. Because although we ourselves had never killed anybody, we'd imagined our ex-husbands' deaths enough times. That's the only kind of murder we *knew anything* about!

If your imagination takes you somewhere and you know the

ground, go for it. Otherwise, don't go barging in where you don't belong.

—

There's another variety of point of view, the *concrete* kind, and you'd think it would be easy to master but you'd be wrong.

My friend and I had managed to wangle a second *Barnaby Jones* episode. We had Barnaby in a strip-mall parking lot. There are some bad guys in a jewelry store. Barnaby sees them; they don't see him. He makes his way across the lot . . . *Wait!* Does he drive? Walk? Run? (He *can't* run; he's too old.) How many people are there in the parking lot? There are two bad guys in the jewelry store: do they just wait, like Tweedledum and Tweedledee, to get captured by the elderly Barnaby? Oh, and how come he can see them while they can't see him? He sneaks up on them, that's why. But how? Where? Maybe we take them out of the store. Maybe we put them in the lot. *But how come he can see them and they can't see him?*

In spite of all the terrible television both of us have seen over the years, Jackie and I can't figure it out. The point-of-view problems have us bamboozled. Jackie's back goes out, and she hobbles away down the hall and into her car. I can't remember how Barnaby managed to catch those crooks.

When I was working my own novel *Making History,* which I firmly believed at the time had transformational qualities that would change the world and make people love each other more (I still believe that might be true if people would only read it), I struggled to get Whitney and Tracie, two endearing adolescent best friends, out of a matinee performance of the

Cirque du Soleil (which took place right by the beach, west of the Pacific Coast Highway). They had to have two other kids in the car, a six-year-old and a baby, and they had to turn north on the highway in order to be involved in a monster car accident, which was going to kill three out of four of them, as well as about a dozen innocent bystanders.

They had to go to the matinee. The circus was important.

The accident had to take place around five-thirty or six o'clock to take advantage of the rush-hour crowd and produce a genuine Los Angeles "sig alert." (That's when all the traffic in the city is screwed up for hours.)

Except that you *can't* turn north, or left, out of the Cirque du Soleil parking lot. You *must* turn right and go up the freeway to the top of the Palisades. I already had a suicidal divorcée up on the Palisades (symbolizing the angry goddess Kali) barreling down Georgina Street, where she was supposed to sail off the cliffs and pancake down on sweet Whitney and Tracie, who had to be down there on the Pacific Coast Highway.

So those girls couldn't turn left on PCH or they'd miss their accident. But the California Highway Patrol felt so strongly about not turning left at that particular place that they'd installed a two-foot-high concrete bulwark dividing the north and south lanes. God*damn*it!

This is what I ended up doing—after, literally, weeks of driving the highway looking down over those cliffs, studying maps, and considering whether it was worthwhile in the long run to deep-six the Cirque du Soleil:

"It was almost impossible to turn north onto the highway," I wrote. "The traffic was fierce. But they did."

Yeah. And the bulwark melted into thin air as I was—once again—defeated by *concrete* point of view, by what you can see and what you can't, where you can turn left and where you can't.

Sex is another milieu that can snag you with its irrefutable rules of point of view.

"She lay back on silken sheets and gazed at him with adoration. His cheekbones, his eyes, his lips, his strangely fragile wrist bones, the three moles clustered together at the small of his back . . ." Except, guess what? If she's looking at his face, she can't see the small of his back. God*damn*it!

My life partner, sweet Mr. Espey, used to amuse himself finding this kind of sentence. One of his favorites was from the distinguished gay novelist John Rechy: "The two guys had lain back, prone, face up, legs spread, butt against butt, cocks pressed together to form one doubled erection . . ."

Well, maybe. Except that *prone* means lying on your stomach, facedown. And even if Mr. Rechy had used *supine,* it would still be a pretty neat trick, about as neat as four people turning left on Pacific Coast Highway during rush hour and cutting right through a concrete bulwark without ruffling a hair.

Wherever you are now as you read this, stop and look up; look around. That's your *physical* point of view. Anything else that you can't see, *you can't see.* It's so irksome. That's why it's tempting sometimes to move all your characters to a planet where point-of-view rules don't pertain. But they're going to have other rules there—even weirder than the ones on earth. GodDAMNit!

Chapter 13

Geography, Time, and Space

GEOGRAPHY

We are framed by our physical world: Geography means parameters: Calcutta or Victorville, a windowless crib in Nogales or a spacious "cottage" in the Hamptons.

Beginning writers love to write about a "man" who gets involved with "a woman" who lives in "the city." When you ask them anything about it, they're apt to get all defensive; they intend their art to be "universal"; they don't want to limit their great work with anything like geography or time or place. By the same token, beginners love to put their characters on mysterious planets, so that they don't have to be worried by the details of what highway you take to get from Columbus, Ohio, to Wheeling, West Virginia. They trust that in "the city," "the bus" will be running twenty-four hours a day, that "the living room" will have "the furniture" in it, and that no character will have to trip over it.

Except that by being "universal" we run the risk of boring our readers to death. Because the "man" and the "woman" in "the city" may be easy enough to write about, but who can stand to read about them?

Think about *place*—the places you know, long for, disdain, the places that frame your life and make you what you are. (And *sure* they can be imaginary; just pay attention to what you're imagining.) Where did you spend your childhood summers? It doesn't matter if it's a stuffy two-bedroom home or a sixty-foot yacht or a public beach or a baseball camp. Were you ever in the service? What was it like? Where were you? (What a difference between Newfoundland, the DMZ, Kuwait, and the bowels of some ship.) How about your first sex? Was it in a backseat? Your parents' bed? A motel?

What's *real* to you? Where would you rather be right now? Where would you most like to never set foot again? (Ironically, those places have a tendency to stick in your mind like flies on flypaper.)

Melville's geography was ships and the sea; Alice Adams's, her beloved San Francisco and her remembered American South. Some writers who don't get out much will never see life except in terms of an English department in a small college, but that's fine: a row of offices, a few modest homes in good taste, toothsome undergraduates around to thicken the plot— if it's yours, it's *yours*. You can't really fake it. You *can* travel places to widen your horizons literally, as Joseph Conrad went to Africa and Christopher Isherwood went to Berlin, or you can stick with what you've grown up with. Think of Larry McMurtry's Texas (he changed his hometown's name, Archer City, to Thalia, but he had to keep the real name of that mean little line of mountains outside of town, Misery

Ridge). Walking outside Archer City in the soft buzzing underbrush, you can almost see where Gus and Lorena pitched their tent, taking those cattle from Lonesome Dove all the way to Montana.

Your world is as important to you as Conrad's and McMurtry's were to them; it had better be, because it's the one you're living in. As Australian Aboriginals might say, if you don't "sing your world into being," no one else will.

A New England city. A father who's off at the war. A woman "alone" struggles to raise her daughters with a sense of dignity and duty. They don't have a penny to their names. One daughter is conventional, another is racked by irrational anger, another is a vain little snot. The one everybody loves the most is doomed to die. *Little Women:* Louisa May Alcott pulled it off, writing not just about what she "knew" but about *where* she was, imagining a family home where ironing and cooking—and dying—could be done with perfect plausibility.

No one else has your information—that's the great part. Your geography cradles your work, rocks it, brings it alive, makes it real.

Your memory is your first editor. If you can't remember it, it may not be your material. How easy is *that*? How many Tijuana bullfights did I watch in my youth, but what I really loved was going to the Foreign Club afterward and listening to the music. That shows up in my work, time after time. (I'm listening to *rancheras* right now.)

Poached fish will never show up in my work, nor will rock climbing, though I've had to eat many fish and climb many rocks.

I'm going to repeat it: Where would you rather be right now? Where would you really, really not like to be?

Sometimes it's hard for me to be honest with myself. For instance, for years I thought—like every other half-baked intellectual on the face of the earth—that I "loved" Paris. Well, sure I love Paris—I'd have to be a bozo not to—but during the time I lived there, and the many other times I've visited, I always felt a keen disappointment. It's awfully cold and gray! People somewhere in the city are doubtless having a good time, but usually they're not me. And it's damp.

Maybe I like Sydney, Australia, better. I *love* it down there! And maybe I love the cranky American desert, although right now I'd really not like to be there. (Except it's great to stop in Baker, between Vegas and L.A., where the temperature is 120 and you know it, because it has the "world's tallest thermometer" and the sky's like a white plate, and there's that restaurant that has the greatest Bloody Marys in the whole world. And you can have two of them, because the dry heat will sweat them right out of you.)

Maybe, more than we like, we're the product of nothing more than bad television commercials. We only *think* we like to walk on the beach. We only *think* we love backpacking. Maybe what we really love is the cement plant, or the restaurant where the waitresses wear white lace hats, or the Foreign Club in Tijuana late at night, with the glittering mirrored roulette wheel and the mariachis sweating and singing. If that's one of the places I'd really rather be, I'm going to have to recognize that before I go forward.

Here's a terrific exercise that has to do with both geography and point of view: Draw a map of where you live, your turf.

You know where your house is, where the gas station is, where the mall is, and—if you're virtuous—where the church is. If you're the adventurous type, you know where the vacant lot is where you once set that fire. But soon—past the freeway, or by the railroad tracks—your knowledge stops. Drawing where you are in the world is marvelously helpful in showing you *where you are in the world.*

If you're thinking of writing a short story with three scenes, it's not the worst idea to scratch out a sketch of the town the story happens in, the living room where people sit and talk, the view from the windows, the traffic outside. All that is part of the story, and the more deeply you take charge of it, the more easily you keep the reader enchanted.

It's nice to know how many beds there are in the bedroom or how far it is from the lake to the river. What does the inside of a mortuary look like when you have to go and make arrangements for your dead mother? Where are you going to bury her? Everyone wants a grave with a hillside view, but what if she dies in Kansas?

If your characters are on a ship, what part of the ship? There's a world of difference between where the captain hangs out and where the people traveling first, second, or even third class like to be—not to mention the crew. (Have you ever, on a "pleasure" cruise, opened the wrong door and come upon a windowless, unpainted interior, stinking of mildew, halls piled up with unwashed towels? It kind of takes the fun out of the Baked Alaska Gala Dessert at the end of the voyage.)

Before you begin to write, you'll be well advised to have some idea of where everything is in your imagined universe. I got myself into a dither that must have lasted a month while I was writing my first novel, involving a Third World spy, an indignant husband, and a pair of glum lovers. I created a motel that ran up against a medium-size cliff in the rough hills of Malibu. There was one driveway in front of the rooms, there were six to eight rooms with no adjoining doors, and there was no room to walk out back, because there was only the cliff with the ocean below; plus, there was no room to turn around at the end of the driveway, so once a car drove in, it had to back out.

I'd done it to myself! Once I wrote the first draft of that scene, it took on an awful reality. I couldn't get the characters back and forth between the rooms. Yes, I could fix it, and after about a month I did. But if I'd given some thought to the geography of it all in the first place, I'd have saved myself thirty days of writing anguish.

Really bad writers don't care about this stuff. They're always having daring adventurers trying to get into "impregnable castles," but then they figure the hell with it and cut to the next scene, where the hero is inside the castle.

We, as "serious" artists, shouldn't do that. If we're going to have a dinner party for ten people, we'd better provide a dining room with ten chairs. If there are only eight chairs, there had better be two people who don't have a place to sit down, or who don't get invited.

More and more, I'm coming to think that geography is as important as point of view. We're always thinking of character or plot and arguing which comes first. But think about it: How much would we care about Dorothy and the Scarecrow and the Cowardly Lion if they weren't traveling down the Yellow Brick Road trying to get to the Emerald City?

TIME

What time is this story or novel happening in? We all know that great work is "timeless," but there's that paradox again: In order to *be* timeless, it had better be rooted in time.

Time is one of the most mysterious and malleable elements in our lives. It's one of the things that make us the craziest, and the most inventive. Watch how spending Sunday afternoon with your in-laws makes time stop; it takes the entire Jurassic age just to sit down to dinner. Or observe how when you're in the hospital visiting a sick person, five minutes turns into eternity. Yossarian, in *Catch-22,* is so convinced he's going to die in World War II that he devises a scheme to do only the things he *hates* so that his life will last longer.

On the other hand, we all know that time is passing us by, that we'll be old before we know it and dead even faster than that. Remember the bell in *The Wasteland:* "Hurry up, please, it's time!" and John Donne's stern warning "Send not to ask for whom the bell tolls, it tolls for thee." We're always trying to beat time or make time, or spend it or kill it. And in the long run, it always outfoxes us. That doesn't mean we don't keep trying, and haven't been trying all along. Let's devour our time, Andrew Marvell advised his Coy Mistress. "Let us roll all our strength and all/our sweetness up into one ball,/And tear our pleasures with rough strife/through the iron gates of life: Thus, though we cannot make our sun/Stand still, yet we will make him run." (And who of us, holding on tight to a lover in a tangle of sheets and sensation, hasn't had the thought "Okay, this is *it,* this is the heart of infinity, I'm not 'myself' anymore, I can forget the ticking of the clock and my ordinary life," but the minute you *have* that thought you're out of eternity and back into time, and the clock is still ticking.

When you're writing, you're God—thank God. You set the time and measure how it goes. When you need to speed it up, you just do it! "Ten years passed," or, "A hundred years passed." When you need to slow down time, you can do that too: Think of Proust taking fifty pages to let his hero turn a doorknob. In Virginia Woolf's *To the Lighthouse,* the first third of the book deals with a dinner party (and time and eternity and longing and the limits of human intelligence), while the brief "middle" flies through time over several decades. The final third picks up those characters once again, still deciding whether to go out to that lighthouse or not.

It's a good idea, on whatever you're writing, to jot the time and place of the scene you're working on in a corner of the manuscript: 10 A.M. on a Tuesday in Liberal, Kansas; 5 P.M. on a wintry afternoon in Paris; high noon in L.A. When? In the summer. Yes, but *when?* I don't know—August?

Let's see: Jennifer is being called for by her date, Howard, at seven-thirty on—Thursday? Friday? Saturday? Sunday night? Those nights mean four entirely different things.

He picks her up at seven-thirty. Yes, but when? Middle of December. Is he freezing to death outside the house waiting until he walks up to her place because he doesn't want to appear too eager? Or is it seven-thirty on a July evening, when the sun is still up, or seven-thirty in April or October? What do those times—those fleeting moments—say about the characters? At the most basic level, they'll be sweating in July and fumbling with overcoats in December.

Oh, screw it! Let's make it seven-thirty in the *morning* when Howard picks up Jennifer. It's the beginning of duck-hunting season and he got a late start, but he doesn't care all that much about hunting; he just wants to be with her out in the country when the air is crisp, and they'll stop at a little place out of town to get coffee and it'll still be early enough to see the steam rising from those cups . . .

Or maybe it's eleven-thirty at night and he's picking her up for a midnight movie. At least that's what he says he's planned . . .

All these thoughts have been about things that happen in what we might think of loosely as the present. The time, I guess that means, when we find ourselves alive. Ancient times come before we were born, and even though we try, we often have a hard time differentiating between old times and very old times. (I see this with my students, who keep referring to Dashiell Hammett and Raymond Chandler in the same terms as Balzac or Stendhal. "Hey!" I'll say defensively. "Sam Spade and Philip Marlowe drive cars and use the telephone—how far in the past can these narratives be?" Their answers, unstated but oh so obvious, are "far, far in the past, further than any of us can ever imagine."

That doesn't stop us (indeed, it often encourages us) from writing about long-ago times. Oh, that fifteenth-century France! How cool was *that*? Except, since there are twenty-four hours in a day and France is in a fairly northern clime, what time did they get up in the morning (if they were rich, or if they were poor)? How much time did it take for the servants or the wife of the house to make a kitchen fire? How much time to make breakfast? How did merchants spend their days? What were their business hours? Was there such a *thing* as business hours? When did people have dinner? How long were they in church? How much time did people spend on spinning, churning, farming, fermenting wine, and in which seasons did they engage in such activities? When was the customary time for lovers to get together, and how much time did they have?

Which is not to say that you can't write about fifteenth-century France if you want to, but if you choose it, you've got to do the research.

You can get delicious hints from literature: Samuel Pepys writing in his diary in eighteenth-century London about trying to get his wife to come to bed with him, but she's busy with the laundry and it's already *two in the morning;* Victor Hugo's French peasants waiting in the street for bread and soup because it takes *too long to cook at home;* or—this from a contemporary newspaper in China—ordinary citizens lining up morning and evening to use public toilets. How long do they stand in line, and how long does the act of elimination take, and what's the small talk going on in that line?

Some writers are great with time: James Jones's soldiers getting bored for long afternoons in army barracks in pre–World War II Hawaii; Laura Ingalls Wilder knowing exactly how long it takes to smoke a ham or ride out a blizzard on the American prairie, and how it feels as that time slips by.

You can try to duck out of some of these worries by putting things in "the future." Ah, the future! People will certainly get around faster (by separating all their cells and re-constituting them again, as in *Star Trek*). Or they'll sleep during the long "years"—would that even be the correct word?—in rocket ships between planets; but how long will that take?

All this is not to make you crazy with self-consciousness but simply to suggest that you scribble (in the margin) in the first draft of whatever you're writing what *time* your story is happening . . . and how long that action takes.

—

Sometimes you'll find yourself writing about something of which you're entirely ignorant. One solution to this is to stop and do some research; another is to blast on through, but *briefly*, so that the reader (hopefully) won't notice.

He shot her.

She shot him.

And (if they're on a boat), blood ran in the scuppers, whatever scuppers are.

Over and out, and on to brighter subjects.

And may I just suggest that most of us don't know as much about sex as we think we do? We know what *we* feel, but that is *it*. Gentlemen: If you ever have the slightest doubt whether those squeaks emanating from your partner have a shaky basis in fact, *speed up!* (not in real life but on the page).

"She shuddered violently, and put her hands on the small of my back."

Thank you. The end.

SPACE

My daughter Lisa recently called to bemoan her fate. "Why don't I work in a bank?" she asked rhetorically. "Why don't I just work as a teller?"

When I asked her what was wrong, she said, "I can't get my characters from point A to point B."

"When you find out how to do it," I answered, "be sure and give me a call."

I don't think it's an exaggeration to say that the besetting headache of my own literary life—whether in fiction or non-fiction—is getting people into the car and out of the car, across the living room and out into the kitchen, up the hill and back down the hill and over to Europe and back again.

I stand in awe of writers who can manage this space stuff—whether it's Tolstoy or Stendhal choreographing whole wars or E. M. Forster managing three respectable ladies, a damp lawn, and only two macintosh squares to sit on.

When writing fiction or nonfiction, the space is all in our mind, and the mind, besides being creative, is irrational and disorganized. It's hard to figure out "space." Suppose I have five young men going to a funeral in the same foreign car. (It makes me shiver just to think about it.) Five guys won't *fit* in the average foreign car. But they're just not the kind of guys who would drive in a big Oldsmobile. Maybe I could put them in a sport-utility vehicle, but suppose they're all jazz musicians mourning a colleague of theirs who's dead of a heroin overdose? Finally, it's probably better to pare it down to four guys—easier in the long run. Or cut out the funeral. Or change their occupations.

Again, although I hate to say it, I have a feeling that men "do" space better than women, or at least more easily, because they've had aeons of getting out and about. Male thought was responsible for transporting Hannibal's elephants out of Africa and through Europe and over the Alps and back down into Italy. Men are always advancing and retreating from something or other.

You can make the constraints of space work for you: Iris Murdoch in *Under the Net,* one of the most wonderful novels in the English language, invents a hapless hero who, along with his equally hapless sidekick, feels that he must steal a German shepherd, a movie-star dog named Mr. Mars, from an invidious villain. Mr. Mars is in a cage in the villain's living room. The cage is too big for the door. A cab is waiting outside. Time is of the essence. The cage could go through the door if it were turned on its side, but when that happens, Mr. Mars's paws go through the bars. Those five or six pages of gorgeous fiction say more about space, existential acts, and the random quality of the universe than all of Sartre and Camus combined.

Time and space have been addressed by writers and philosophers time and again. You can go back to Aristotle for a refresher course on observing the "unities." Or you can even use the phrase "Aristotelian unities" in conversation if you want to scare people.

But I would suggest that while we keep an eye on those rules, we can have a hand in making up new ones. This world is stranger than our Greco-Roman, Judeo-Christian, mainly European culture would have us believe. There are other dimensions than the same old three we generally fool around with. Distance in Montana is different from distance in New York. In Namibia or Thailand, time may be different too.

How do geography, time, and space play out for *you*? Sometimes, when I have trouble with time and space in my own novels, I comfort myself with the idea that I'm looking at a far more complex universe than the one Hannibal confronted when all he had to do was get those elephants over the Alps and sneak down behind the Romans.

Chapter 14

Building a Scene

Over and over since I've been working on this book, I've been making notes to myself: Don't forget to tell about eating raw broccoli or drinking black coffee or dancing around the room to raise your energy level. Or, Should I mention that a very famous novelist masturbated thirteen times a day when she was writing—should I pass that information on? Or, Should I mention that it's not necessarily drugs and drinks per se that people object to; it's the bad behavior? You can actually drink a fair amount as long as you don't begin your sentences with "You think you're so smart. Well, let me tell you something . . ."

But should I pass this information on, and if so, where and how?

And how many times have I written down "Pray to the universe—*you're* not the one doing the writing"? But do I do a whole chapter on the Divine, which, though I know It's there,

I know nothing else about? Do I divulge that I pray to the Virgin, Kwan Yin, and Kali?

Over and over in my notes I find "building a scene"; don't forget "building a scene."

But does it lend itself to a whole chapter, this building-a-scene business? It's just something to keep in mind. If you're a playwright, you're, by the nature of the genre, stuck in a scene. You've got a stage you're working with, and actors on it. You can play with that structure, have your actors wear masks, or say what they're *thinking,* etc., but you've got human beings locked to the stage by gravity, bound by inexorable rules of time. Your work is guaranteed to be grounded in *scenes.*

In novels, nonfiction, magazine pieces, learned essays, you're working in different media. Not to belabor the obvious, but you're playing around with print, black marks on a white page. You're attempting to a) get a vision out of your own mind and soul, and b) into the reader's mind and soul, via the printed word. Our minds are prone to flights of fancy, so some of our prose tends to *fly away.*

Sometimes this can be great, as in James Joyce spending time frying kidneys up in a skillet. But even the most extravagant flights of fancy—in the hands of the masters, or the un-masters—are grounded in scenes: Proust's doorknob, or Joyce's cramped kitchen, the urine-tinged aroma of frying kidneys.

It's so obvious that it's hard to talk about. It doesn't deserve a whole chapter, certainly. But without a demarcation of scenes, your work isn't going to make much sense. (And by demarcation I just mean: First there's one scene and then another and then another, and so on, until the end of your work.)

You set up a scene: "Magdalen was in the bath when we arrived. We went into her sitting room, where the electric fire and the little piles of nylon stockings and silk underwear and the smell of face powder made a cozy scene. Finn slumped onto the tousled divan in the way she always asked him not to. I went to the bathroom door and shouted, 'Madge!' The splashing ceased, and she said, 'Is that you, Jake?' "

That's Iris Murdoch again, in her exquisite first novel, *Under the Net.*

Murdoch, remember, was a distinguished philosopher, one of the great minds of her time. But she's writing a novel here. Jake is telling the story; he's got a sidekick called Finn, who (we can tell by page 7) is an enigmatic fellow. Magdalen is one of Jake's girlfriends but not the one who matters. None of them are rich. They're all friends; they've known one another forever. But Madge has decided to marry a bookmaker, and Jake kicks up a fuss about it. They tell Finn to leave, and she and Jake make their (temporary?) farewells to each other. "If you come back when Sammy's here," Madge says to Jake approximately a thousand words later, "he'll break your neck."

Jake, thrown out of Madge's place, strolls, parcels in hand, to "a newspaper shop in the neighborhood of Charlotte Street," where a proprietress, Mrs. Tinckham, chain-smokes her days away in the company of "an ever-increasing family of tabbies." Mrs. Tinckham hands him a stack of manuscripts from a French author, whose work he translates, and approximately 1,500 words later, Jake breaks out of that scene to address the reader.

"For the purposes of this tale, I have shattered nerves," he says. And then adds that he spends a lot of time with Finn: "I am thinking perhaps about God, freedom and immortality. What Finn would be thinking about I don't know." About 750 words after that, Jake snaps back into the newspaper shop scene, leaves most of his things with the old cat-lady, and embarks on what will become a profound and hilarious existential quest.

When you start a scene, you need a place, and some characters who are going to do something, and then the scene—often approximately a thousand words—is over. Something will have happened.

In the best of all possible worlds, each and every one of your scenes will have a perfect purpose, perfectly realized. But in a writer's life, this doesn't always happen. Christopher Isherwood talks, in one of his Berlin stories, about sitting in a squalid room with a couple of other people wandering in and out and he's trying to write. One of his characters says to another, "Why are we so unhappy?" And, of course, the author can't figure out what to write next.

But you don't know until you write the scene whether it's going to work or not or if you'll need it later. The main thing is, when you start, give the reader a break and let him know where your characters are and who they are (poor Jake, with his shattered nerves; the imperturbable Finn; that airhead Madge, who's smarter than she lets on). Try to manage to have something happen, and then STOP. Get out and move on. When you feel the need for flights of fancy, try to make sure that they're grounded somehow, some way, in a scene. Try to avoid that moment when you're sitting at a desk with a sweet person who's line editing your work and he looks at you and says, "Could you explain what you were doing here in pages eleven to seventeen?"

And you take a look and it doesn't mean a damn thing and you say, your voice made up equally of despair, defiance, and fear, "Isn't that . . . stream of consciousness?"

———

That's all I know about building a scene—that you'd better be aware of it and that you'd better be prepared to do it.

And . . . that raw broccoli has some ingredient that wakes up your brain and that dancing around the living room when you're stuck puts oxygen in your blood and lifts your spirits, and that God *knows* what that famous lady author was doing but that her work was undeniably great, and that the universe is the one who really writes our stuff, but that doesn't necessarily mean the crabby old Divinity with the long white beard, and if you must drink or do drugs be sure to bathe a lot (notice that they call it "clean" when you stop), and try to maintain a ferocious graciousness, perfect good manners.

If I were editing this chapter down into "scenes," I'd take out the broccoli, drugs, dancing, divinity, solitary pleasure, and just leave the information on scene-building, with its references to Iris Murdoch and Christopher Isherwood, and maybe throw in some material about Patrick O'Brian's Aubrey/Maturin series, twenty wonderful novels set in the late-eighteenth- and early-nineteenth-century Royal Navy, in which Jack Aubrey, the cheerful man of action, and Stephen Maturin, the mysterious intellectual, chase around in marvelous ships, participating in the Napoleonic Wars, eating and drinking too much, eluding capture and getting captured, inflicting injury and getting injured, falling in and out of debt, riches and love, in scene after glorious scene.

But I think I'll leave this just the way it is: what some of us think about as we're trying to build a . . . you remember!

Chapter 15

Rewriting

Just looking at that dreaded word gives me pause. *Rewriting.* Or *revision.* Such overtones of penance: *rewriting!* It's what they're always telling you to do in Freshman Comp classes, and your work never gets better; it always gets worse. Teachers are always marking the margins with cryptic comments like "a little awk," and sure you know it's a little awk, but what the hell do they expect *you* to do about it?

Revision—what scholars are continually doing in hope of publishing some dreadful derivative scholarship they've put together in hope of getting some pointless promotion or tenure: "I'm revising my dissertation on Ralph Waldo Emerson's 'common cold imagery in the latter essays' . . . ." Or, "You can't go out and play until you've *rewritten* this paragraph a thousand times!"

Revision is when you first get to recognize the distance between what you wanted to write, what you thought you were writing, and what you actually did write. That recognition often makes you want to throw up.

But all that nausea means is that your work could stand some fixing. It's not as horrible as the teachers of Freshman Comp would have us believe.

—

First, three reminders; then, four steps (which should take you fairly easily through four drafts. By that time, your manuscript might stop making you sick and start to make you happy).

REMINDER ONE

I hate to even suggest that you'd be doing this, but don't plagiarize. (I plagiarized half a sentence in the "Point of View" chapter.) Some people have the urge to do it, like engaging in kleptomania or unprotected sex, but it's bad for you. You always get caught, or if you don't, you'll always be worrying about it. Also, editors and/or professors who consider themselves tolerant to the point of radicalism cannot tolerate plagiarism: It brings the outraged moralist in all of us to the fore. If you—even accidentally—plagiarized, now is the time to take it out.

REMINDER TWO

Don't revise for more than two hours at a time, especially in the early stages. Two hours is plenty. All kinds of studies suggest you shouldn't ever do more than two hours worth of anything—driving on the freeway, exercising, you name it. After two hours of concentration, your brain begins to short out. If you're up against a deadline, you'll find yourself working longer, but there's no virtue in it. In fact, the act of revision can be so stressful and weird, especially at first, that sometimes one hour is more than enough.

REMINDER THREE

My own anxiety level is so high during the early stages of revision that I've sometimes resorted to an unhealthy anti-anxiety diet: a cup of Campbell's tomato soup, taken with a glass of harsh red wine. Often it's very hard to sit in one place and read your own cruelly imperfect work. Tomato soup and red wine dull the impulse to jump up. Pretty soon you don't care how awful the first draft is. You can keep your eyes on the page for minutes at a time, which is all anybody is asking you to do.

—

There's no one right way to rewrite; I can only tell you how I do it using these four steps.

FIRST

• **Respect Your First Draft!** Back in the days of typewriters, tormented writers had a lot of fun writing half a page, then yanking it out of the typewriter with a gigantic *rip*, balling up the paper, and hurling it in the general direction of a wastebasket. A floor covered with wadded-up paper was a fine measure of integrity and artistic temperament. Now that drama doesn't pack the same punch: Poking the DEL key on your computer is a bleak little gesture.

I'll repeat: Respect your first draft! It's your child, just a little uncoordinated and unkempt. Don't throw that baby out with the bathwater. The fact that you wrote it makes it significant. You must have been trying to say something, even though the manuscript may look like subliterate Sanskrit to you now.

When your first draft is done, your first step is simply to read it through. If you find word-for-word repetitions, you can cross some of them out, *a word, a phrase, a sentence at a time.* If the words *proceed, rather, quite, rancho,* or *sour cream* appear five times on one page, you can cross a couple of them out. If a paragraph makes absolutely no sense to you, just write *fix?* in the margin and go on reading. Have a little glass of wine. Or some tomato soup. All your meanest demons will be raving as you're reading your first draft.

Why not revise as you go along? Some people do, but my own general insecurity and confusion are so high that if I revised as I wrote, it would take me ten years to get a page done. Also, I don't want to start revising until I know what I'm revising *toward.*

SECOND

• **Make a "Map":** As I begin my second, more "serious" reading, I can't help but see just how awful the first draft really is and how chaotically my mind works. I see the same scenes coming up over and over, the same pointless flash-backs, the flashbacks *within* flashbacks, the author intrusions where I treat the unsuspecting reader to four- or five-page treatises on the injustice of it all. They're so "beautifully writ-ten," in my mind at least; too bad they have absolutely noth-ing to do with anything.

And although there is a beginning and an end in there some place, the middle tends to be undifferentiated mush. That's due to two factors: I'm generally more interested in character than plot, and I have the habit of writing my first chapter, then my last chapter, then the second chapter, then the penultimate chapter, then the third, and so on. The middle, for me, is al-ways a mess.

Here's my way of making sense of it (and this works equally well for magazine pieces, fiction, and nonfiction). It sounds like a lot of work, but it's no worse than shelling enough peas for a dinner party for six. I take out some blank paper and a hard copy of whatever it is I'm working on, divide the blank paper vertically, draw another line across the top, and label it thus:

Ch. One

What I Have	What I Need

Then I take a look at my troublesome, chaotic, emotion-packed, repetitive manuscript. Oh well. Nothing to do but start.

What I Have	What I Need
pp. 1–2½ Club description We first see Claudia	Who *is* Claudia?
pp. 2½–4 Flashback, Singapore, the old days	pp. 2½–4 Where'd that nightclub go?

I just keep going. Say it's one of the last seedy nightclubs in Singapore. The government wants it closed. Claudia, a haggard but beautiful American woman, enters hesitantly, flinching under the hostile/indifferent (?) eyes of the local expatriates. She's promised to meet a handsome Swede (at least he said he was a Swede). But why'd he pick such an awful place to meet?

What I Have	What I Need
pp. 4–5½ Blather on Far East	pp. 4–5½ Cut? Fix?
pp. 5½–6 Sven enters	pp. 5½–6 Cut this dialogue

Ah, the blather! How I love to go on about the mystery of long, dark bars, the exotic secrets of an entirely made up "Orient." My first husband wasn't Eurasian for nothing! I get lost in damp silk shirts and Singapore Slings, opium, Tiger Balm, humidity. Alienated Caucasian losers.

But here's something I can't help but notice: I can't do a Swedish accent. I just want a lanky blond guy. So he either has to stop talking or change his nationality. But now's not the time to worry about it! I'm just writing down *what I have* and *what I need*. If it's a twelve-page story, maybe my map will run a couple of pages; I'll break it down by paragraphs. If it's a novel, maybe this map will run ten or twenty pages. But by the time it's done, I'll have a very clear idea about what's going on in this 280-page manuscript, a clear idea of the places I've repeated myself, where I've left out very crucial information or put in things that absolutely don't work. This includes motivation (while driving on a Los Angeles freeway during rush hour once, I literally broke out in a sweat because in my third draft of *The Handyman* I realized that the only reason Angela would run off with Bob was because I wanted her to. When I got home, I poured myself a glass of wine, went to my map, and there, in the last chapter, when Angela leaves with the handyman, under "What I Need," I wrote, shakily, in capital letters, WHY?).

So, then—this is still the second step—I read the manuscript again, but with my map beside me. I can fairly easily let that blond guy come from Northern California and stow that terrible accent, and I can have some fun with the sanitized-fascist streets of Singapore. But I try to cut out the blathering!

Let the story tell itself!! Which is what I tell my students a dozen times an hour, but of course the one who really needs that advice is me.

Now is the time to begin cutting—*judiciously*—never yielding to the temptation to tear the whole thing up because it's so far from what I thought I was writing.

I keep reading, no more than two hours at a time, and crossing out (or adding) a word or paragraph at a time. After a while, the items in the right side of my column will get crossed out; they'll get "fixed." If I go away from the manuscript for a couple of weeks, I won't have such a hard time coming back to the project, because *I'll have its map right there,* available to me in ten or twenty pages.

I'll find things that aren't strictly necessary to the narration but they're my very favorite passages; they sound so *cool*! I know those lines don't belong there on page 34. Maybe somewhere else? I deal with this in the old-fashioned way, with scissors and tape, cutting out the paragraphs in question, putting these strips into an attractive folder marked MY FAVORITE STUFF. I take these passages out and read them regularly. Sometimes I can squeeze them back into the story; often I can't. But they're still there, in that purple folder, and maybe a scholar will find them someday.

My third step—and this is because I don't work from an outline; I feel it hems me in—is to make a one-sentence summary of what goes on in each chapter. I usually do it in a very primitive way, with boxes.

THIRD

- **Chapter Summaries:** Switching to my earlier novel, *Golden Days:*

1.	Edith and Harvard by the beach	10p
2.	Scene in yacht club	20p
3.	Selling jewels to matrons	11p
4.	Bomb falls	20p
5.	Flashback to 1951	15p
6.	After the bomb	45p
7.	Meeting Skip	10p

I do that until all the chapters are listed. In my own mind, the ideal novel is twelve chapters of thirty pages each—not that I've ever managed such a thing. Each chapter is like a short story or a unit of some kind.

I know that in each of my "literary" novels the chronology has radically changed during revision. In almost every case the chapters, especially in the middle, end up getting switched around. Because—forgive me if I'm hazy on this—the story that I'm telling and *the story that I'm telling* are two different things.

In *Golden Days,* which had to do with the end of the world, my first few drafts had things pretty much starting at the beginning and ending at the end. It took me hell's own amount of time to realize that *the world had already ended* when the story begins. Maybe your story will get told better if it comes in a different order. What I generally do is print out all the chapters, put a little note on top of each one with its summarizing sentence, and arrange them all on the kitchen table. Then I stand around and basically look at the chapters for about a week. I put chapter 7 over there, where chapter 10 once was, then stand back and think about it. And think about it some more.

Once I really do have the *chronology* down the way I think it should be, I do another

What I Have	What I Need

outline, or "map," but not as detailed as the last, because I'm beginning to know the book pretty well.

And then I read it through a couple more times, and read it through again.

Do I know enough about the characters?

Do things make sense?

Are there any outrageous mistakes that I keep glossing over hoping they're just my own delusions and nobody else will notice them?

If I've done that much, then I've done the best I can. As my old Texan dad would say, an angel can do no better and a donkey can do no worse.

FOURTH

• **Fine-tuning:** Anybody who went to a parochial grammar school knows that there's a difference between linking verbs and action verbs and passive voice and active voice. If Sister Cletus were here, she'd tell you that strong verbs make strong sentences. So when I look at the verbs in my sentences, are they good and *strong*? Do they hold my sentences together? The passive voice is really good for only one thing: the weaselly notes in committee meetings where nobody wants to get blamed for whatever happened: "It was decided, after much discussion, to request the resignation of Mr. Edgemont," or, ". . . to deny all collateral damage in the last military action." Are your sentences in the active voice for the most part? ("Ms. Jones said that Mr. Edgemont exposed himself to her for the fourth time during the noon hour. Tom, Phil, Hadley, and Sara all agreed that this was finally too much. Edgemont gets the ax on Monday A.M., soonest.")

Look at your sentences one at a time. Do they appear clean and seemly, with a regular subject, verb, and direct object? *Do they make sense?* That's more important than the most eloquent and lyrical embroidery.

Finally, what about the *words*—each and every word. It's not for me to say whether your diction should be plain or fancy, but it's not a bad idea for your words to match your subject. For instance, people expect presidential inaugural speeches to be made up of semi-biblical blasts of hot air. This is an important country, the presidency is an important job, and the inauguration is an important occasion. A recipe for sponge cake employs one kind of diction, the report of a football game another kind entirely. I like a plain style myself, but that's only personal taste.

Here's another thing: Every writer has a set of "favorite" words, words that break out in his or her head like a bad case of hives. For years I could never get a character just to "eat a hamburger." He would have to "proceed to eat a hamburger." Then he couldn't just "wash his hands" afterward. He would have to "proceed to wash his hands." It was a tic! It was a disease! It was like one of those carnival games where a wooden gopher pops up and you whack it with a hammer but then another wooden gopher pops up: *Proceed! Proceed! Proceed!* But at least, once I realized it, I could proceed to control it. Or at least try.

The repetition of "favorite" words is potentially enlightening. What is it about our own brain that kicks up some words and not others? The late Tommy Thompson, whose *Blood and Money* is one of the most fun and gory true-crime accounts of all time, finally decided to write a serious novel, and because he was an American guy, odds are he probably thought he had at least a reasonable chance of writing the Great American Novel. I can't remember the name of the book, but I do remember that he used the word *espied* (instead of *saw*) *twenty-three* times in about 440 pages. In all his down-to-earth, journalistically wonderful nonfiction stuff, people just "saw" each other.

Alison Lurie, at the beginning of her career, remarked that in some workshop a fellow writer had pointed out to her that she used *rather* rather a lot. It seems to me that *rather* is a lot like *proceed:* It shows a tentativeness, a shyness about whatever it is you're trying to write, an unwillingness to proceed, if you will. Once aware of it, she stopped using *rather.*

John Espey's particularly favorite word was *relish,* used as a verb. When he and Lisa and I were collaborating on the Monica Highland novels, he'd begin a sentence, "He relished the . . ." and Lisa and I would tease him, shout him down: "No more *relish*! This isn't a hot dog!"

A few weeks ago, going through his papers, I found a six-page short story, a fragment, really, that John had written for an obscure literary quarterly in 1959, years before I knew him. It was a morose tale of a depressed father (since he was going through a clinical depression at the time) taking his kids on a hike, where they see some condors. His sadness was so palpable in the story that it broke my heart. Then, from forty-one years ago, when I was twenty-six and hadn't even met him yet, this sentence: "He relished the sensation of the whiskey taking hold of him, and closed his eyes."

Oh, sweet person! Sweet person who wanted nothing more from life than to enjoy himself a little, to *relish* it and impart that sense of fragile enjoyment to someone else . . .

I don't want to get too sentimental about it. I've read a couple of thrillers lately where someone gets to "tidy up" after dead bodies six times and another where, in a jungle of decaying corpses, the word *riparian* turns up three times. What can it mean?

By one of life's amazing tricks, we often can't see our own favorite words. They are so much our favorites that they become profoundly part of ourselves: Everyone else in the world notices Grandma's bright blue eye shadow, but *she* doesn't see it. She's been putting it on every day for fifty years; she doesn't even notice it.

So about now is the time for me to ask a trusted friend or relative to take a look at my work. I try to be specific about what I want from them. I absolutely don't need their opinion about whether my work is "any good."

I *do* need them to:

1. tell me whether or not things make sense.

2. track whether every character has the same number of relatives at the end of the work as at the beginning. (No two children increasing to three or decreasing down to one.)

3. point out any tiresome repetition of *scenes* or *phrases* that I haven't noticed.

4. tell me about those "favorite words" that stick out from the narrative and call attention to themselves. (I mean, *riparian*. Really!!)

My reader, or readers, will be able to tell me this without having to say whether I have a great future in literature or not. And with luck, I'll be able to return the favor of an intelligent reading if they attempt some work of their own.

———

If you've gotten this far, you're ready—maybe—for a last couple of readings. There are two dead giveaways that separate the dilettante from the straight-up writer. The dilettante absolutely won't accept suggestions from an editor; the dilettante gets all pouty and retreats into rhetoric about "integrity": "I'll never change *which* to *that,* goddamnit! I have my integrity!"

And the dilettante quits work before he or she is finished. How tempting it is not to do the last round of work on a piece, so that when it gets turned down, you can say to yourself, Well, it wasn't my best work anyway.

The straight-up writer makes some strong coffee and goes through the piece (the chapter, the book) one last time. How do you know it's the last time? When you don't have any more notes; when you don't feel sick to your stomach; when everything you've written "fix?" about is fixed; when you can turn page after page and nothing jumps out at you. You do it and do it and do it until it's done.

It's not necessarily going to be the happiest occasion in your life. Because once you finish, there's a moment, a heart-sinking moment, when the world you created is cut off from you forever. You can't get back in that world in exactly the same way, ever again.

Oh well! It's done.

Now you need to print out several perfect copies (and make copies of your disks as well). Now you need the highest-grade paper and the best printer you can get your hands on. Now, if you're the praying type, is the time to pray. Now is the time for charms and blessings. Now is the time for the perfect package—I love lavender or gray manila envelopes for magazine pieces—and the finest stamps at the post office; get ones that mean something to you.

Now is the time to send it out.

And if it comes back, get out your charming-note stationery.

PART III

During, and After

Chapter 16

That First Trip to New York

When you get off the plane it's always damp, whether it's winter or summer. The cabdriver—if you take a cab into the city—speaks a language you can't understand, and the last name on his license is unpronounceable. You're hurtling along a highway between some of the ugliest row houses you've ever seen: Who could possibly live in a place like this? Why would they want to do it?

Then you cross one of the bridges and there really is a change in the air, in the level of energy. It's still damp, but there's a hectic, shivery thing going on, and you pass all those little, dinky businesses shoved up against each other, fruit stands and flower stalls and coffee joints, and it looks so old-timey somehow, so small and funky and uncared-for; there's certainly no point in being afraid of *this,* is there?

If you're lucky, you have some friends, and that's where the cab will let you off. They'll take you in and hand you a drink or a cup of coffee. But even if they've got money, chances are their apartment will be something like the size of your dining room at home. Their doors will have about six or seven layers of bright enameled-white paint with plenty of cracks and the bathrooms will have those tiny white tiles in octagonal arrangements that were old at the beginning of the last century.

If you stay at a hotel, it will be glitzy in an old-fashioned way (gilt and fresh flowers at the Plaza) or seedy in an old-fashioned way (dead air conditioners stored in the closets at the Gramercy Park Hotel) or trendy in an embarrassing way (no dresser drawers in the rooms at the W, and *grass* growing out of the bench in front of the elevators) or appalling as only a New York hotel can be: hand towels thrust into holes in the walls at the unrenovated Royalton to keep out entrepreneurial rats. Air shafts and soot and blank walls and windows that won't open.

None of it matters—squalor or luxury or the kindness of friends or the meanness of strangers—because if you're like me, you go to sleep the first night in a sweat of desperation and wake up the next morning with a knot of dread, because you're in New York City. You think you're a writer; you've got a few appointments and plenty of time between them; you've got to make some phone calls now, have breakfast (and try to keep it down). Then you've got to leave the relative safety of this room—even if it does have a hand towel sticking out of the wall—and go out on the street and find some transportation and get to somebody's office and figure out the elevator system and manage to get upstairs to the fifty-third floor and wait with dignity for a while (as you get a chance to realize that everything you're wearing is wrong) and . . .

The person you've made the appointment with has never heard of you, or maybe he has and you'll leave that office with the chance of a new agent or a magazine assignment, or you will have met a book editor you think you like, or you will have had a dazzlingly brutal rejection; but guess what? You're still alive and the brute who rejected you had a nice sprinkle of dandruff on his shoulders. Maybe the next person will take you to lunch or open up a little office refrigerator to give you some Perrier or encourage you to write a piece for him on spec or ask you to give him an outline, or she'll go out of the room for a minute and come back and say, "Sure, you can have the assignment. No more than two thousand words, and can we have it in a month?" And . . .

You go out on the street and lift your arm and a cab miraculously stops, and at the next place—let's say it's *Esquire*—a man comes out of his office to intercept you in the waiting room and say, "Miss, I've read your tear sheets and honestly I can't think of one reason on earth why you should be writing for this magazine," but you wait until that asshole has disappeared back into his office and you go down to the *next* office and come out with an assignment, so that . . .

When the well-dressed lady at *Glamour* and the bepearled agent who used to work for the Kennedy clan tell you that you're totally unsuitable for whatever it is they had in mind, it really doesn't matter, because you've survived a day in New York, the repository of all your hopes and dreams, the place where big-time publishing lives. Your dreams have some reality now. Those names you've only imagined have physical bodies attached to them, and some of them are actually nice; some of them are swell.

So you may go home high as a kite, or it may go badly and you may slink back lower than a toad, but when you sit down to write thank-you notes to all of them, at least you know whom to love, or hate. You start saving your money and planning for the next trip, thinking that next time you'll remember to get tickets to see a show or visit the Museum of Modern Art, or go uptown to see the Cloisters or down to check out that Statue of Liberty because, what the hell? You belong in New York as much as the next person.

Don't you?

—

Maybe this is a time to talk again about finances. Your travel expenses, hotel bill, cab fares, restaurant tabs, and *part* of your clothes (as "costume") are deductible on this trip to New York, and you'll be sure to have an envelope with the dates of your stay written on it, where all the receipts get tucked in for you to add up when you get home.

Where are you going to get the money in the first place? I've already talked about a "writing account," but here's another way of looking at it. When I was broke—"We are the kind of people," a friend of mine once said haughtily, "who may be broke from time to time, but we are never poor"—I went to an "alternative" financial adviser, who suggested that I break down my assets this way: Think of keeping four accounts, he said, four different places to put your money. It doesn't matter how much money. Do it like this:

Ordinary Checking	Travel Account
Large-purchase Account	Permanent Wealth

I know I had some reservations at the time. I could barely afford peanut butter. But the adviser—admittedly, one of those optimistic California types—said this: "As long as you keep working off a scarcity consciousness, you're never going to get out of this jam you're in. You already have an ordinary checking account, so you've got one category covered. And you're paying off a mortgage on a house, so you can think of that as building some 'permanent wealth.' The 'large-purchase account' is for stuff you can't afford—a water heater if yours blows out, a beautiful new dog if you feel like it, or bicycles for the kids. If you don't like a bank account, start with a jar. The travel account is for dreams! For wherever you want to go!"

That was how I worked it when I was a broke single mother. It was a way of playing, of learning how not to be scared (because I had been the kind of financial moron who had "let my husband take care of everything." I never even wrote a check until after my divorce). But, look! If you were a writer, you could play with that paradigm a whole other way.

Ordinary Checking	Travel Account
Literary Expenses	Permanent Wealth

Forget the dog and the water heater! What you really need is money for good stationery, helium balloons, chocolates, flowers, and clothes for New York, which are different from the outfits you wear in Flagstaff, Columbia, Denver, Miami, and L.A. The "travel" money goes for New York. Every day you write your thousand words or revise for no more than two hours, put a dollar in the travel jar and a dollar in the literary-expenses jar. It's not so much—far less than you'd pay for a decent margarita!

At the end of a year—or two years—after you've been planning that trip to New York, you'll have money enough to at least approach the project. (Put another way, you'll have fewer excuses not to go, because you'll be closer to being able to afford it.)

Why does a writer even need to go to New York? Isn't the whole point of this book how to make a literary life *wherever* you are? Yes, but New York City is where the publishing world is, where the magazines are, where they hand out the literary awards and listen to ideas for stories and draw up the contracts. So you have to go there. (Just as, if your heart were set on writing for television or the movies, you'd have to come to L.A., just for a visit, just to sit in on some meetings; and you'd be wearing a different set of clothes and staying in a different kind of hotel.)

Think about it *before the trip*. What do you want from New York? It's such an Oz there, such a wonderland, it's hard to know where to start. Even if you weren't a writer, you'd want to see a couple of plays—right? Maybe hit the Guggenheim Museum? Walk in Central Park? Go shopping along Fifty-seventh Street? Go down to the Village on a Saturday night? Maybe you want to have a few drinks in a glamorous bar; maybe you want to meet the love of your life or just get lucky for a night or two. These are things you can write down on a list without going into a cold sweat of fear—civilian things.

But if you've been writing along for two years, or five, and sending out your charming notes with determination and élan, you'll have begun to have some working knowledge of American literature and where it is today. You'll have acquired an idea of what it is you want to write and where you'd like to be in two more years, or five, or ten. Suppose you have fifty pages and an outline of a novel. You'd like to find a publisher for the damn thing. Perhaps you love three or four magazines, read them all the time; you've sent notes of appreciation to several of their editors. You've sent each of them a piece or two (which they've probably turned down, and you've responded with a charming thank-you note). So you'd like to pay a social call to, say, three magazines, just to say hello and see if you can get an assignment. While you're at it, you'd like to meet a couple of agents to see if you can get someone to represent you.

And you have a couple of friends from high school who you think are living there now; it might be fun to look them up.

Just writing these last three hundred words has put me into a sweat. New York is so damn scary! But you plan your trip one day at a time, think about it, obsess on it. Buy a map of New York. Look at it, the way you looked at maps of Paris in your high school French class. It's *where* you're going! You can put up the map somewhere on the wall with a dazzling affirmation or two. (That's what Henry Miller did when he was saving to get to Paris—he had maps of that city on paper, on hand towels, and souvenir hats; there was no *way* he wasn't going to Paris, broke or not.)

Begin thinking about *when* you're going to go. Unless you're some kind of hardy Midwesterner, you don't want to be in New York in the winter (although it does look good at Christmas, I admit). You don't want to go in high summer, because you'll melt and everyone's on vacation. Late March and early April are great, because green things are beginning to push out of all that gray snow and New Yorkers are in a good mood. October is wonderful, because the fall brings an edgy energy. That's good, because you're going to be stretching your own limits of courage as far as possible.

How does your work fit in, if at all?

You've already got what could be loosely called, in your dreams at least, a correspondence with a handful of editors. Now's the time—maybe as much as six months ahead—to write, very casually, "I'm planning a trip to New York in October. I'd love to stop by your office and lay eyes on the person who's been turning me down. I'll have ten ideas and pitch them to you in eight minutes or less!"

It's very possible they'll say yes. If they say they plan on having intricate back surgery the whole month of October, then you can consider postponing your trip to April . . .

The "text" here may look like a drama of yearning and rejecting—you're doing the yearning and the editor is doing the rejecting—but it's really a narrative of courtship. He's the girl; you're the guy. Are you reliable? Do you do what you say you're going to do? (Do you say you're going to write a piece about turkeys drowning in rainstorms and then, three weeks later, send it to him? Will you be gracious when he turns it down?) Do you persevere? (Will you keep letting him know, politely, that you're in this for a lifetime?) Are you darling? (Is your stationery beautiful, your penmanship correct, your prose style perfect?) Are you smart? Do you have something he wants? Do you make him laugh? Maybe he won't want to get married, but chances are he'll give you ten minutes of his time, especially if you mention it to him six months in advance. And tell him about your novel, even if he's a magazine editor. People change jobs all the time. The main thing you want from this first trip to New York is just to put some faces to some names, to make acquaintances, get the lay of the land.

———

It's time to start making lists in earnest. You want to have *money* for:

> airfare
> cab fare
> the hotel
> restaurants
> theater tickets
> staying out late in bars

You need a list of *fun places to go:*

> Elaine's (very hokey!)
> The Russian Tea Room (hokier still!)
> one high-budget Broadway play
> one low-budget off-Broadway play
> a museum or two, maybe

And a list of *everyone* (civilians) *you know or ever knew in New York who:*

> you were ever married to
> went to high school with
> are cousins, uncles, etc.

And a list of: everyone you've ever written to in a literary capacity:

> writers
> editors
> magazine people
> agents

If you have a book, you want to be sure you have fifty pages and an outline in perfect shape.

If you're visiting magazines, it's great to have a couple of identical sheets of paper listing ten ideas for pieces, each summed up in three or four single-spaced lines. Hold one in your hand as you pitch stories to the editor, and hand a copy to her as you leave, so she has a ghost of a chance of remembering who you are.

You also need a list of *every contact you've ever made:* at writers' conferences, extension courses, or night classes on writing. Get on the Internet; track these people down. If they live in New York, write them a note and tell them you'll be in New York for eight days in, say, April. Are they available for lunch? Breakfast? Coffee? Tea? Drinks?

Besides your list, you'll need a schedule. Little by little, it will fill itself in. Say you fly in Wednesday and leave on Sunday . . .

Wed	Thurs	Fri	Sat	Sun
	__	__	__	Church
	__	__	__	Leave
	__	__	__	
	__	__	__	
Fly in	__	__	__	
Dinner	__	__	__	

Notice: You usually save hundreds of dollars in airfare if you spend Saturday night in town. I'm not a churchgoer, but New York is teeming with churches filled with pageantry and fancy choirs, and you may be in a mood to thank God before you leave. Your first night should be spent just by yourself, or with the people you came with—a time both to get grounded and to allow yourself to be thrilled and excited. Obviously, if you're a twenty-four-year-old guy, you may want to see what kind of debauchery you can scare up, but you also want to go easy that first night: New York dread and a terrible hangover make a ghastly combination.

The blanks will begin to fill up: Friday-night dinner with an old friend; Saturday afternoon at the Museum of Modern Art with your aunt, who's coming over from New Jersey.

Then, oh, yikes, yikes, yikes! It's time to follow up your notes with a phone call to an editor you've been in touch with, and it's a good idea to *write down* when you're going to be in New York and exactly what you have in mind ("I wonder if I could take you out for a drink on Thursday the eleventh or Friday the twelfth?"). Write down your name and phone number (because, I'm sorry to say, I've been in a position on the phone to New York where I've forgotten both those items of information).

If this schedule seems overwrought or just too pathetic—as in what kind of pathetic loser would have to make such detailed lists and dig up old friends that he or she hasn't seen for years and even write down what he or she's going to say on the phone?—I have to state: The pathetic loser that *I* am, okay? The one who *still,* on the phone to a New York stranger, has to keep from saying: "I'm Carolyn See?" in the form of a question, as in, "If you don't like my name, I'll be glad to change it for you." And if I put together an elaborate, overly thought-out schedule, it's because the alternative is lying down on a hotel bed and staying there all day, thinking, *This is a terrible mistake, all of it. Whatever made me think I could do any of this?*

New York strikes terror in my heart because it's my most basic flash point, where my dream of what my "literary" self is smacks right into intransigent reality. My persona is one thing when I'm at home—I'm living a life of the *mind*, right? It's my mind. I can think what I want, love what I want, in the privacy of my own mind. But somewhere, on the way over one of those bridges that take you into Manhattan, my dream crashes into REALITY. What if they hate me? But nothing bad that anybody ever says to us is as bad as what we can tell ourselves.

If you have some money saved and some good people to see; if you've chosen your time well—fall or spring; if your proposals and outlines are in order, you could very well be a Buckaroo Bonzai kind of person, who courageously aims his rocket ship at that brick wall and, by a combination of work, determination, and white magic, blows into another dimension.

In that dimension, transubstantiation occurs: The life of your mind is made flesh. Sometimes it's a nightmare. When Lisa See, John Espey, and I wrote our first novel as Monica Highland, we went to New York to discuss the advertising budget of *Lotus Land* at our publishing house. (We'd been told they wanted it to be a big, flashy bestseller.) We were ushered into a boardroom and stayed there for quite a while until people began to file in. Strange, they were all "girls," twenty-three or under. Then a man came in and said there *was* no budget. The whole imprint had closed down; we were to be their last title. Again, we were the rats who *hadn't* been given any vitamin C, and the scientists wanted us to die pronto so that they could get on to the next experiment.

That was a nightmare worse than our worst nightmare. (Nothing to worry about. We took some desperate measures and that sweet book got translated into a dozen languages, and we met some people who would change our lives for the better, but while it was going on, it was bad.)

On the other hand, recently, as a member of the board of the Modern Library, I found myself having lunch in a private room in a New York restaurant and I got to sit next to Shelby Foote, who writes so wonderfully about the Civil War. "There are two great disgraces in American life," he told me. "Slavery, of course, and then the way we walked away from the problem of Emancipation." Yes, I thought, *and I'm sitting here and you're telling me this.* On the other side of me the next year was Jon Krakauer, tanned and dazzlingly handsome, drinking martinis and grinning a perfect grin, as happy as I was, I think, to be there. I couldn't help thinking that once again I'd lucked into the very heart of Infinity, where dreams manifest into spectacular reality.

These moments happen all the time in New York—the good ones and the bad ones. You get to have them, and you get to live through them. Soon enough you'll be going back to live in your mind, at home, but not now.

———

Clothes are not my forte, but I can say that people don't dress in New York the way they do in the rest of the country. All those platitudes one used to read in women's magazines— about less being more—absolutely don't hold true in this city. Remember how they used to tell you, if you were a young woman, to get dressed to go out, then stand in front of a mirror and take at least one ornament or accessory *off*?

Women are different in New York. They *swirl* a lot, in layers of boots and stockings and short skirts and long skirts and coats and cloaks and scarves and pearls and cameos and Mother's good jewelry and more scarves and tortoiseshell clips stuck in their (beautifully coiffed) hair. It's quite amazing how they do it. Another kind of New York woman wears black, beautifully tailored suits. She favors single strands of very good pearls. As a general rule, these women are thinner even than women in Hollywood. (At one meeting I'll never forget, I couldn't take my eyes off the woman across from me; she was dressed in beige silk, with breasts so small that her sternum was the main thing that poked out of her blouse.)

I admire all this more than I can say, but I don't think there's a way an outlander can emulate it. You can play with it, though. Whenever something black and expensive goes on sale in your hometown, you can buy it up and put it away in tissue paper for "that trip to New York." You can eschew all unnatural fabrics and stick to wool, cashmere, and silk. You can browse antiques stores or estate sales and pick up anything that looks as if it might have been Mother's best jewelry. You can save up for the finest possible pair of black boots or pumps and a black leather bag that looks as though it cost a fortune. There's an underlying seriousness about the way New York women dress; I don't think I'm wrong when I say that anything flamboyant or inexpensive worn on the female body would be taken by literary New York as low or disrespectful. All that is something to be kept in the back of your head: If you see some black suede gloves on sale but you live in Albuquerque and it's heading into spring, buy them and put them away. You'll need them as something to wave around and strip off when you get to New York.

For men, I think that a beautiful suit and several ties—Peter Jennings's ties—are it. If you're from the West and incredibly proud of it, you can go the Western way: I once had dinner with a famous white-haired Western attorney/writer who carried about thirty thousand separate pieces of chamois fringe across his barrel chest, along with a passel of Mother's best turquoise jewelry around his neck and Daddy's best cowboy boots adorning his he-man feet. But unless you're a cowboy, I wouldn't try it. They're serious about clothes in New York: the best suit you can afford, the best shirts you can afford, the most exquisite ties you can put your hands on—as well as all the litter of winter accessory gear you can think of.

You won't fool anybody for a minute. At the end of my last trip to New York, I stood outside my hotel in a black silk blouse and black wool skirt, nice black boots, a real Ferragamo purse, a string of great pearls that might have been Mother's best, if she could have afforded any. A Pakistani cabdriver put my suitcase in the trunk, handed me into the car, gave me a huge smile, and said, "*California?*" Well, sure. I couldn't even fool a Pakistani cabdriver. But just as when you go to a foreign country and blunderingly ask, in the native language, "Where is the station railroad, blease?" they appreciate your effort. It amuses them. They look upon you kindly.

One last thing now that you're in the taxi to the airport: Remember to save enough money for that cab! It pains me greatly to remember this, and far more to admit it, but during that last drive on my first trip to New York, I realized I wouldn't have quite enough money to pay the driver. Young California fool that I was, I told him so. He pulled over to the side of the road and pitched me out into some weeds. I had a long, humiliating walk to a sleazy motel in the middle of nowhere, where I cried my eyes out to a notably unimpressed audience of strangers and finally managed to hitch a ride on a shuttle bus. Not an experience anyone should go through.

And save a few more dollars for a couple of Bloody Marys on the flight home. You'll need them.

Chapter 17

Getting Published, Part II

Here's one of the saddest, most exasperating parts of my life as a writer/critic.

I get a phone call from someone I've never heard of. "You don't know me," he or she says, "but a friend of a friend gave me your number. I have this book; I've been working on it for ten years. It's finally been published, and my editor said that since the pre-reviews weren't very good, there's nothing they can do, or at least that's what somebody said the last time I talked to anybody there, and there haven't been any real reviews, and my editor said they were going to give me a party, or at least there might be a party, but now my editor is fired, I guess—at least he won't answer the phone. They said what my publication date was going to be and I told my family, but my aunt called from New Orleans and her bookstore didn't have it, and my mother up in Maine said her bookstore never heard of either the book or me. So . . . they said you could tell me what to do."

"Did your publisher send out bound galleys to the major newspapers and magazines?"

Silence. Then: "What's a bound galley? I'm not familiar with that term."

"It's an early printing of your book—the *galleys*—that they bind in a paper cover and send out to critics and people they think might give you blurbs."

Silence. You know they're thinking over the word *blurb*.

"You can usually tell how interested the publisher is in your book by what the bound galley looks like—if it, you know, has a good-looking cover or if they have some marketing plans listed on the outside. Did anyone tell you about the first printing, what they were planning?"

"No."

"Well, you might want to call the publisher and see if they sent out bound galleys."

"I *told* you. My editor either isn't there or he won't answer the phone."

"You'd be calling the publicity people anyway. What's the name of your publicity person?"

Silence.

"You might want to find out, and then call up and ask. You might have to send out some copies of the book yourself."

"How am I supposed to find out who the *publicity* person is?"

"What if you call the company and ask the receptionist who the head of publicity is? Then hang up, wait an hour, call again and ask for that person."

"Those are long-distance phone calls."

"Well. After the first phone call, why don't you write the publicist a letter? Or why not call the newspaper in the city where you live, ask for the book-review editor, and see if they've received a galley. That's not the same as asking for a review. Tell them you're just checking."

Silence. Somehow or other, all this has become *my* fault.

"How do I find out who the book-review editor is?"

"How about calling the paper and . . ."

"They *promised me* a party. Now they won't answer the phone."

"Give your own party! It's totally deductible! And all you need is some cheese and cheap wine, some plastic glasses . . ."

"Where would I give it?"

"Your neighborhood bookstore, I guess. Ask the manager and tell him you'll take care of the invitations . . ."

"How do I find out the manager of my bookstore?"

"You go into the store and ask to see him. Then you introduce yourself."

"What about the invitations?"

"What *about* them? You go down to Kinko's and get them printed up, or do them on the computer, and get your mailing list . . ."

Sometimes, after as much as an hour of this pitiful jabber, I have to ask, "When did this book of yours come out?"

"Last October."

"But this is August!"

"I told you, there haven't been any reviews and nobody has even *heard* of it! That's why I'm calling you!"

"When did you say those pre-reviews came out?"

Another silence. "What *is* a pre-review anyway?"

What am I supposed to say? Am I supposed to be like the pet merchant in the Monty Python skit who says to his customer, "That parrot's not dead, it's just in shock"? Because in this case, the parrot in question is not in shock; it's *dead*.

—

Commercial publishers have a "list," which is divided into four parts: fall, winter, spring, summer.

The fall list is always the most prestigious, so it's good to be on a fall list, in theory. The downside is that your little book is competing with the work of the best-known writers in America.

Winter is problematic. Conventional wisdom says that nobody buys books after Christmas. On the other hand, your chances for serious reviews are better, and your likelihood of ending up on at least regional bestseller lists are far better.

Spring is okay.

Summer is for amusing reads, beach books—in theory. If your book has a lot of sex and silliness, it's wonderful to be on a summer list. All that silliness shuts down in September, when the big literary guns come out again.

But take a look at this: What do all these lists have in common?

They only last three months! Because three times four is twelve, and there are twelve months in a year, and that's it. If your winter books haven't been sold off the bookshelves in three months, they get "returned," which means the stores pack them up and send them back. Then they get "remaindered"— i.e., sold again somewhere at a huge discount—or "pulped"—

i.e., shredded. So if you wait four months to wonder where your reviews are, your parrot's dead.

For most serious nonfiction books or literary novels, only two or three or five or six copies will be sold in any given bookstore. If they don't get sold in three months, they're *out* of there! I've spent a lot of time in bookstores. I've seen cartons of books come in and not even get opened; the sellers just stamp them RETURN and they go straight back out the door. (This is particularly true of books that publishers have already wishfully designated as "bestsellers.")

Now, there are all kinds of exceptions to these marketing rules. After your three-month shelf life in stores, you can sell your book to clubs and discussion groups and off the Internet. But let's take the conventional approach for now.

—

The fate of your book is decided, as far as the publisher is concerned, months before publication, at the company sales conference. Writers are often never told about sales conferences, because what is your editor supposed to say? "Guess what! Your book has leukemia!" He's not going to call up and tell you that you're getting placed far back in the catalog or that your first printing is going to be fewer than ten thousand—or fewer than five thousand—and that your bound galley is going out with a cover of dull mustard-yellow. Or that they're going to skip the bound galleys and just send out the typescript. Why would they want to tell you? The editor probably feels as awful as you would if you knew about it. This isn't doing anything for *his* career either.

Your destiny is further settled two to three months before your publication date by three "pre-reviews": one from *Library Journal;* one from an outfit called *Kirkus,* and one from *Publishers Weekly.* Which publication you think is most important generally has to do with which one gives you the best review.

Two out of three of these publications are shrouded in mystery. In all my life I've never put my hands on an actual copy of a *Kirkus* review; I only get reviews of my work clacking in over the fax machine. But *Kirkus* has a grand reputation for integrity, for not being besmirched by commercial concerns. *Library Journal* is supposedly revered by librarians, and libraries buy a lot of books. Or not. *Publishers Weekly* is the hard, unsentimental trade journal of publishing. Its pre-reviews carry enormous weight, especially if they're negative. Conversely, to get a "starred" review means a lot, and to get a "boxed" review means the world. (It doesn't mean you have a bestseller, though. It just means that for the rest of your life, your book will have had a boxed review in *Publishers Weekly.*) "I saw it," my editor sputtered when my novel *Golden Days* got a boxed review, "sitting there on the page like a big yellow cab!"

But most of the time your editor isn't going to call you. You may not get a very good review—because nobody ever heard of you or the reviewer is in a bad mood or who *knows* why?

Your fate has been tweaked earlier, in a series of moments when the sales rep for your publisher meets with the buyers for bookstores. Those sales reps don't have the easiest life in the world. They drive hundreds of miles a day to take their two or three "lead titles" on that season's list and ram them down the bookstores' throats. They're often not going to spend much time on weeny little books toward the back of the catalog (which is why your cousin in Seattle probably won't be able to find your book).

Finally, right around your publication date, when even the most experienced and cynical writers are prone to sitting around waiting—against all previous evidence—for their lives to change, your book should be reviewed, at least by your local newspaper. (Here, New Yorkers have an inestimable advantage, since their local paper is *The New York Times*.) But, notoriously, reviews have a tendency to not come out in a timely fashion. They either show up before your book is in the stores, so that potential customers can't find it, or they appear in the paper just after the stores have returned your book. The review is often bad—or, even worse, tepid—or it's short or stupid or the reviewer didn't get it.

Oh well!

It will all be over in three months anyway, this part of the publication process, because the thing to remember is that—in terms of reviews and bookstores—the life of your book is directly comparable to boysenberry yogurt. Open your refrigerator right now; take out one of those little yogurt cups and put it next to your printed-out manuscript.

There you are.

Even though our work is sterling, ground-shaking, extraordinary, etc., not too many other people are going to share that view *automatically*. (The other night, at a book signing, a very sweet lady volunteered from her folding chair, "*Golden Days* literally changed my life! It told me to be a better person!" I can't tell you how much that cheered me up, but within about thirty minutes, from other statements she made, I couldn't help but notice that the woman was stark raving mad.)

———

After you write your book, *you* must sell it. The three months before and after publication are just as important as the years you spend writing. People may help you with this process, but you are the one who's ultimately responsible for the reception of your book. Not your publisher or your agent or *anyone else* is going to do it for you. Because, think: When you have a baby, who's supposed to take care of it? *You* are the one! You can abandon it or hand it off to foster care or an orphanage or a spinster aunt, but that baby won't thrive. It needs its mommy or daddy! Nobody else cares as much as you.

The astounding ignorance shown by that phone caller at the beginning of this chapter is not ignorance at all. It's the same thing that keeps "traditional" wives from knowing how to write checks or guys from knowing how to work the dishwasher. The instinct behind this "learned stupidity" is: If I don't know anything about it, then I won't have to do anything. Because if I do something and it doesn't work out, I'll suffer more than I can even imagine. Paralysis is my best policy!

Five months later, you begin to have desperate thoughts— CPR thoughts. You call friends of friends on the phone.

———

Remember the *mailing list* you've been working on for months or years? Hopefully, it's in a computer file. Hopefully, it can be broken down into cities or zip codes. (Don't go all *dumb* on me now!) Three months before the pub date of your book is the time to sort out the list. These are the people who should know about your book. They include—again—your old professors and schoolmates, your carpet cleaner, the guy who fixed your roof. Before you say, "Oh, I couldn't ask them," think for a minute. If these people aren't going to buy your book, then who on earth *is* going to buy it?

In your own town you'll have enough addresses for a nice invitation list to a party. (Here in L.A., our family likes to throw two parties—one on the Westside, at Dutton's; the other at Vroman's, in Pasadena—because this is a big town and hard to drive through.) Do you have clumps of addresses from other major cities? Enough for a few reasonably well attended book signings? Good.

When Terry McMillan realized, after the disastrous publication of her first novel, that her publisher wasn't going "to do anything," she wrote letters to every black church in America when her second book came out and arranged for readings. She knew who her potential readership was, and she gave them a heads-up. Look at her now.

Every person on your mailing list should get an announcement or an invitation to a signing or a party. The announcements can be fancy or cheap—it really doesn't matter.

The bookstores in your area should carry your book. No one else is going to assure this but you. That means, six months or even a year ahead of your pub date, you should make it a point to go into the bookstores in your neighborhood *just to make friends*. Introduce yourself and say you have a book coming out. You'll probably meet a lot of disaffected, miserable, minimum-wage employees, who'll look at you as if you have a live frog in your pocket, but pretend you're back in high school. You have to "make friends" with these people. Pretend you're having a good time. Chat.

Chat, goddamnit! You can't let these people go on being strangers. You have a book coming out. They have to know you're there. Many of these sad-seeming strangers are book lovers, who may actually read your book and then actually *sell* it.

Write "charming notes" to people heading up service clubs, churches, what have you. Tell them you have a book coming out. Do they need a speaker at any upcoming events?

Somewhere around this time, three or four months before pub date, you and your editor will have a talk about *blurbs*. He'll call up, sounding bored. "Do you, uh, have any idea of anyone who's ever written anything who might want to put in a good word for this book?" Now is the time you thank God for those charming notes you've been sending out all along. You will have names and addresses of writers you admire. You can have your editor ask *for* you, or you can screw your courage to the sticking point, pull out your good stationery, and write them a nine-line charming note, the only favor you'll ever ask them. If you can remind them that you bought this book and that book of theirs and had a wonderful conversation with them on such and such a date, chances are really quite good that they'll come up with a blurb, even if it's only:

> "Smart, funny, sexy.
> The best I've read in a long time."

Around this time, you want to send a letter to your editor, with a copy to the head of publicity, saying how pleased you are about everything and what *your* dreams and wishes are for this book. Try to stay within what we laughingly refer to as reality. Go easy on requests for advertising. They love to say no to things like that. Concentrate on what *you* can do to facilitate the publication of your book. Mention your mailing lists, the organizations you've called, any contacts at all you might have in radio, local TV, or newspapers.

It goes without saying that you will already have set up your own website. People love it when you have a website already set up. It's the one place where you can take the position that you're king (or queen) of the world and nobody will argue with you. Look at other authors' websites; take a computer class and start doodling.

Every writer wants a *book party;* publishers hate to pay for parties. The feeling seems to be that the party does nothing except make the author feel a little better about life and that's not the business the publisher is in.

In fact, this is absolutely the time when an author needs to feel better. We throw housewarmings and birthday parties and baby showers and bachelor parties; we need parties when our book comes out. The way I've dealt with it for years is to say, in my letter to my publishers: I'll pay for a party in L.A. if you'll do something in New York (because I have to hold my head up in my own hometown, and it has to be more than cheap wine in plastic glasses).

Guess what? The odds are your publisher will say, "Oh, we really discourage you from coming to New York. The competition is terrible here. There's no media to do. People here don't come out for parties, blah blah blah." Don't have a tantrum about it. If you don't know anybody in New York, throw the best party that Cleveland has ever seen.

If you feel that you know enough people in New York to put a party together, I'd say, *Go for it.* Pay for it, fly there, stay up late, party. Send invitations to everyone you can think of. (By this time, you should have a passing acquaintance with some people at magazines or black-shirted denizens of the Village or people you met when *they* were out on tour.)

I went through the proverbial tortures of the damned when my novel *Rhine Maidens* came out. The publishers began telling me I was "distinguished"—i.e., that they weren't going to spend a cent on me. And *especially* that I didn't need a party in New York. I wept. And wept some more. Then I remembered: They didn't own me! I sent out invitations, flew to New York, and invited the people at the publishing house to come along if they wanted to. It was a great party. Once I got there, people were very nice. (Don't try it if you don't know enough people in New York, though.)

—

I've been thinking about book reviews. In spite of the fact that I've been a weekly reviewer (first for the *Los Angeles Times* and then *The Washington Post*) for longer than some of you have been alive, the process remains largely a mystery to me. This is what I know. A few months before your publication date, your publisher will send out those bound galleys, or sometimes just photocopied manuscripts, to book reviews and reviewers around America.

I know some people would disagree with me, but I believe that if you haven't seen a review in the papers you daydream about by one month after your pub date, you're justified in sending copies of your book, with *very* unassuming charming notes, to the book editor or the columnist or the journalists you'd love to have pay attention to your work. You can just say, "I'm dismayed about this book of mine; I fear you haven't received a copy. If you have, please accept this extra one, with my best wishes."

I don't think you can do this, if you live in New York, to *The New York Times*. It would be like tugging rudely on the Ark of the Covenant and saying, "Hey! Pay some attention, will ya?" But editors at other papers will open your package and sigh and maybe give your book a second chance.

The main two things to remember, though, are:

Four months after your book is published, it's dead. Send out your requests in a timely fashion.

Also, remember your good manners! Whatever reputation you have or end up with will become inextricably combined with your bad behavior. (That basketball celebrity who ran for the presidential nomination a few years back made his book-publicity ladies cry. Who'd ever want *him* for president?) If word gets out that you're a maniac, it's not going to be good for you in the long run.

By the same token, it's not cool to go into stores, demand to see copies of your book, and then fly into a raving fit if they don't have it in stock. An alternative is to take a few copies into a store. Shake hands with the person across the counter and ask if the store has some in stock. If it does, try this: Buy two or three copies, sign them, *give* them to whoever is working at the store at that time. Offer to sign the rest. Say you hope they like it, smile, and leave. They'll remember your courtesy.

If the store doesn't carry copies of your book, stow the tantrum! Pull out a few from the bag you're carrying, inscribe them, shake hands, give them to the salespeople, and leave. (Don't worry about the expense; it's deductible.)

Something else: First-time writers love to buy copies directly from the publisher, taking advantage of the 40 percent author's discount. Don't do this! Everything you buy from booksellers is reported on the computer, and helps you get on the bestseller list. Everything you don't buy from the booksellers is not. When you're selling—particularly for the first time—they don't expect miracles from you. They may *hope* for miracles, but they really just hope for decent sales. Sales of hardcover books, for the majority of authors, number in the single thousands, sometimes even—month to month—in the hundreds or the dozens. One way or another, as a working writer and snoopy person, I've been able to get my hands on various publishers' spreadsheets that report sales from week to week. Some very famous writers might sell only eleven copies across the entire country in any given seven-day period. This is true. Any of us with some decent friends and relatives can do that well. But in order to be recorded, these sales must be *counted on computers in bookstores*.

Three last things to say before I'm done with this chapter, and I don't mean to be unduly pessimistic when I say them. First, everything that can go wrong generally *will* go wrong. Second, you may have to take desperate measures. Third, after the book comes out, you're going to go through some serious postpartum depression.

—

Everything that can go wrong *will* go wrong! Don't worry about it. If you go to a book signing and there are plenty of people, the books won't be there. If you go to a signing and find a hundred books to sell, there won't be a person in sight. If you write a book called *In Detroit*, some joker will be sure to write a book called *Out of Detroit* within three months. If you go on tour, there's going to be at least one tour stop that will be a branch of a chain store in a neighborhood with nothing but aluminum-siding businesses, or the bookstore will share its parking lot with the baseball stadium and a baseball game will be going on. Alison Lurie spoke to eleven people in Los Angeles at Dutton's. Jamaica Kincaid spoke to eleven people at Book Soup in Los Angeles. I sold a bundle of *Making History* in Philadelphia one year, and three years later I had an audience of three—one of them was flat-out drunk, draped artistically across five (otherwise empty) folding chairs.

They'll lose your luggage, you won't have a hotel room, and the review of your book won't appear in Minneapolis until two weeks after you've left town—and a week after the local stores have returned your books.

Sometimes the whole situation calls for desperate measures. Suppose you're frantic for some *public relations*. But you can't afford a public-relations person. You need someone to write press releases, because you know a press release about your career and various projects would be just the thing to get you some interviews or some kind of coverage. You'd love to be interviewed by at least the local newspaper, but you just can't make that phone call: *Hi. Would you like to interview me?* You need a P.R. person in a big way, but not only can you not afford one, your town doesn't even have one.

And you want to send a press release to *Publishers Weekly* because you've dreamed for months or years about getting your name and the name of your book into that magazine, but your publisher's publicity department—if indeed there is a publicity department—won't take your calls. You feel like you're drowning, like you're the rat in the experiment that didn't get the vitamin C.

Let me flash back, all the way to the sixties in Topanga Canyon. It's a warm Sunday morning, we're drinking coffee on the balcony, looking out over acres of chaparral, and suddenly we see a naked lady doing yoga. It's just wonderful! I'll call her Mary Helen Hazelton.

Flash-forward five years. I'm broke. I really need a P.R. person. After a couple of weeks of agony, I take a desperate measure. I go down to Kinko's and create some stationery for "Mary Helen Hazelton and Associates" with a post office box and my own phone number. I write some dazzling press releases and send them to everyone I can think of. I see not only my name in *Publishers Weekly* but the name of my P.R. person, Mary Helen Hazelton. She's doing a wonderful job for me. And I do very well impersonating her on the phone.

After the book comes out, I more or less forget about Mary Helen. I'm able to afford a real P.R. person for my next book. Then one night on the six o'clock news I see a hauntingly familiar, very pretty face. There's a caption underneath it: MARY HELEN HAZELTON: PAST-LIFE THERAPIST. *She's so darling!* In some ways, the best P.R. person I ever had.

—

It's three months after pub date. Except for some talks at ladies' literary lunches, it's almost over. Publication of this book didn't change your life. Even if it did, it didn't change your life the way you thought it would.

If it succeeded wildly, you may be getting a lot of uncharitable thoughts coming your way, a general feeling that you didn't deserve it. (Oddly, this feeling may originate with you.) But more generally, even if the book's "coming out" process has gone very well, even if you've been fairly reviewed, sold a decent number of books, and met some literary people you'd only dreamed about before, it's going to be over, it's almost over, and then—*God*—it's over. You're back to your same old life. You're a person who wrote a book once. (And everyone knows critics hate a second book.)

Your life does change, but it's like plate tectonics or subatomic particles: These changes aren't usually visible to the naked eye, the vulnerable brain, the aching heart. But your position on earth has changed and will change as you go on writing, as you become acquainted, gradually, with your literary self. Others will get to know that self as well. Every time a stranger—or a friend—reads your work, your life is changed, the world is changed, whether you know it or not. And while a book's commercial "selling" life is three months, a book is hard to get rid of: It sits on shelves in the homes of your mother's friends; it will get picked up when someone has the flu; it bobs up again, drowning but perky, on remainder tables. It may change somebody's life after all. I once had a casual romance with a pretty awful novelist and took one of his paper-backs along with me to a session with my respected therapist. This bad novelist was so unimportant to me that I hadn't even mentioned him in my long list of grievances about life, but my therapist sat up straight, pointed to the book, and said his name out loud. "I'll owe that man a debt of gratitude forever!"

"Why?" I asked. Because he was really a bad novelist.

"I had foot surgery and I was in the hospital in terrible pain and somebody brought me that book. For four hours I didn't think about my foot at all."

That man's dead now, but we know that for four hours—*at least*—he made the world a better place.

Whether your world or *the* world is changed or not, a terrible sense of loss prevails when the publishing process is over: postpartum depression.

Your editor will say, "You should be working on a new project," but I've never known anyone who could do that right away. You worked as hard as you could on something, with all the hope in the world, all the anxiety, despair, and dedication you ever had or dreamed of having, and the work, the book, the story, the project, is gone, lost, past.

Like a loved one in a blurred photograph.

Oh well!

Time to start looking at the world like an artist. Again.

Chapter 18

Magazines, Grants, and
Fun with the Tax Man

After all that work with the book, after the flashes of ela-
tion and sickening disappointments you've been through,
you're going to need some money.

If you're not a bona fide "bestseller," money comes in a variety of ways. You can teach "creative writing" (if some institu-
tion will hire you), you can do the occasional book review, you
can give inspirational speeches (if anyone will consent to listen),
and you can sell some books out of the trunk of your car. All
that is fun. But money for the serious—and even frivolous—
writer flows to you basically in three ways: by applying for
grants, doing magazine pieces, and having some fun with the
tax man. You can go on with your day job if you're lucky
enough to have one—T. S. Eliot was a banker; William Carlos
Williams was a doctor; etc.—or you can go looking for "a big
advance" with your big-advance truffle pig, but only a true
maniac would expect to make money from writing short stories or literary novels.

Writers are divided naturally into two groups: those who prefer to write grants and those who thrive on doing magazine work. They have two entirely different mentalities, as different as Democrats and Republicans, and neither is more right or wrong than the other. The grant people come under the general heading of "Somebody, somewhere, owes me a living." The magazine people snarl in tough accents, "Quit your bitchin' and get a *job*!"

In reality, most writers do both, and treat their income tax forms as poetry.

I hate to apply for grants (although I've been lucky enough to get some wonderful ones). To me it seems too much like begging to be entirely comfortable. Also, I've judged many applications and have seen way too many distinguished writers grovel piteously for dollars. Really, I don't like the process at all.

It's nice to get the money, though!

When you're thinking of grant applications you need to be storing up two kinds of data in your computer. The first is a working "bio," the story of your life organized by chronological accomplishments. Include your birthday and when you graduated from whatever school. List the places you've worked, leaving out the boring jobs and keeping in the interesting ones. This biography is, or should be, a highly polished work of art, showing, *by dates and places,* the kind of person you are. This is one of those times that if you've been in jail or you come from Mombasa or you have eight children, you should *include* that material. As in any first draft, overwrite, then cut. Keep hard copies around and a working copy in the hard drive.

The second item you work on is your résumé or bibliography. Keep a record of everything you've ever published, every award you've ever received, every conference where you've spoken. Think of your résumé as your report card to God. Writers create these in different ways. I like to keep my résumé on one page. I abbreviate and truncate and shorten and edit, because I like the way it looks. But I've seen poets, for instance, who carry around twenty-page résumés, dog-eared: every last line they ever wrote, lists of every out-of-the-way wretched village where they've made an appearance. Whatever style you like is fine. But you should have this material handy at all times.

The third part of grant writing is usually a personal essay, or a "statement of plans," which explains why the people who have the money should give some to you. I would just say that this section in any grant gives judges the opportunity to make some mean fun of you. It's absurd to expect them *not* to repeat a juicy piece of gossip, especially if they know your work. I'm going to give one example. God knows it could apply to dozens of writers, so I'm not giving away any secrets. A young male novelist, in one of his grant applications, allowed as to how he'd been lying on his stomach, in bed, for the last two years. He didn't get the grant, but five judges—his peers—know more about him now than they should, and won't ever be able to read his work in the same way again.

Your personal essay or statement of plans should implicitly, and maybe explicitly, suggest that you're a genius, that you're on speaking terms with the Larger Universe, that you know exactly what you're doing, and that they'd be *lucky* to give you the money. It's not the worst idea to write the first draft of this under the influence of drugs or alcohol, because a few delusions of grandeur aren't a bad idea in this context. The main thing is to keep the groaning and grievance to a minimum.

Because, contrary to what you may think, they *don't* owe you a living.

When you're finished, edit the application rigorously, bless it, mail it, send it on, and *forget* it. If it works out, fine. If it doesn't, it doesn't.

But keep all that material safe on a computer disk; you'll be able to use it again.

—

Writing for magazines has always seemed more rational to me. You're selling a product, and if you get a rejection, they're only turning down twelve pages, not your immortal soul. Also, magazines continually need writers; they have issues coming out every week or month—they've got to fill their pages with something.

Think of those charming notes you've written to writers or to editors. Surely some of them have given you a civil answer. Think of some of your favorite magazines—leaving out *Playboy* and *The New Yorker*. (They don't need you!)

What magazines do *you* pick up? Put another way, what are you interested in? It doesn't have to be world peace or motherhood or highway safety or anything terribly grand. Everything under the sun is possible material for a magazine piece.

In an undergraduate class, I was preaching this doctrine when a sweet youth was imprudent enough to say that all he was interested in was beer drinking, *heh heh!* By the end of the course, he'd written a piece on "designer" beers and had sold it to an in-flight magazine for a few hundred dollars.

There's a huge difference between getting a Guggenheim, which can support you for a year in a dignified manner, and finding three hundred dollars in the mail for a piece called "Best Brewskies," but there's something very nice about that $300 or $700 or $3,000 or $7,000. Those dollars are real. They're like tips from a night of waitressing. They're like getting cash for mowing the lawn. The dollars don't say you're a "genius," but they say, very reassuringly and definitively, that you can write and that somebody will pay you for it. (They're the opposite of MFA programs, where you pay somebody else in order to "learn" how to write.)

By and large, magazine writing attracts the young. The editors you may find yourself writing for often go on to more prestigious jobs with book publishers. Your first magazine editors may end up being your lifelong friends and associates. I had a dear neighbor in Topanga Canyon years ago who loved nothing more than zooming around on his motorcycle; now he lives in New York, has a great shock of silvery hair and a scholarly stoop—he's an editor at a fine publishing house—but when I see him, I still see him in his crash helmet, and I know about the tattoos beneath his pin-striped suit.

Here are a few things you might write about: Travel, anything from an around-the-world jaunt to the one-hundred-mile trip to see your wife's parents. Camping. Life in RVs. Sexual function. Sexual dysfunction. Good kids. Bad kids. Your weird childhood. Your happy childhood. Whales. Fishing. Hunting. Cooking. Tequila. Keeping a neat house. Keeping a sloppy house. Sleeping pills. Hamburgers. "Profiles" of anybody you happen to know. Alternative medicine. How you got cancer and got better, or didn't. Whatever you're interested in *now*. That's the other thing: A magazine piece will only be in your life for a few months. It's only practice, muscle building, keeping "fit," in the literary world.

Don't send the editor a query letter! Remember—he's wired to say no. I do think it's a good idea to write a couple of notes establishing yourself as a fairly wonderful person and showing a shrewd understanding of the publication. Then write a note saying you're working on a piece you'd like the editor to take a look at; you'll be sending it along shortly. Then send it along shortly! Three or four weeks later, write him another note saying you hope he liked it, but if he didn't, that's okay: it's your lifelong ambition to publish in that magazine's pages.

Again, there's no query in any of this. You're proceeding like the very best of seducers, assuming that it's a done deal. The editors would have to rouse themselves to say, *No! Send us nothing!* But human beings are often too torpid to rouse themselves.

—

Now I'm going to tell you how to write a magazine piece. First, never write anything longer than twelve pages. (That humble piece of information is worth the price of a hundred copies of this book.) Keep it down to ten pages, or eight if possible.

Second, consider that the traditional magazine piece is divided into four parts.

Part one is some kind of vivid scene, written in the present tense, illustrating what you're writing about. If you were an English major, you would call it the controlling image.

Part two is what I call the it-was-not-always-thus section. It's where the "back story," the history, comes in.

Part three is whatever you're writing about: the action, the story.

Part four ends with a knock-them-out, bring-them-to-tears image: your very best stuff.

That's it!

It's so simple, it's criminal.

Here's one example (a piece I've never written, an experience I've never had, though I've thought about it enough).

Whale-mating rituals in the Sea of Cortez.

• **Part One.** Your tire's gone flat, you've run out of gas on a godforsaken highway in Baja California. The sky is white and merciless. Your friends are cranky. You're drinking a warm orange crush and thinking dark thoughts: How did I get into this? The cacti and caked dust aren't talking. But you know: You're on a quest to see the whales meet and mate in the Sea of Cortez. You've wanted to do this forever.

• **Part Two.** It's been a long time since those whales were first spotted by sixteenth-century Spanish missionaries, and longer than that since the Indians first saw them. But it was only recently that zealous Japanese fishermen almost succeeded in making them extinct . . .

• **Part Three.** But now you're *here.* You find the village on the inland side of Baja you're looking for, check into the motel, meet some other people, order a good meal (whatever the story is).

• **Part Four.** You go out in a rowboat into the sultry waters, close to midnight, in the moonlight. Whales are all around you, whooshing, gleaming, whistling. It's a cosmic experience, and you tell it that way.

—

Most working writers put a patchwork life together. As I've said, they teach a little, do some reviews and essays, a few magazine pieces a year, work on a larger project—the "book." They give talks at lunches. Money comes in expectedly and unexpectedly. This all works together. Most writers are too genteel to talk about it publicly; on the other hand, it's one of the things we talk about among ourselves incessantly: what's a good job and a bad one, what magazines pay well, how nutty some of the editors are. (I had dinner recently with a journalist who was ready to chew up her wineglass because she'd profiled a he-man movie star for a well-known magazine and the editor had the nerve to change the actor's quotes, saying he wasn't "punchy enough.")

"Never again," she groaned. "I'll never write for those people again." But there are plenty of other magazines, other schools, lunch clubs, writers' conferences—an infinity of places to generate money.

—

Once you've got that writing money, though, what are you going to do with it? Hopefully, you keep putting five, ten, twenty dollars a week into your writing fund, a nice little piece of change that can come in handy when you take that second trip to New York or when your next book comes out.

But the best way to feel—*what?* Happy? In control? Gleeful?—about your writing income is to have some fun with the tax man. I should make it clear here that I am not qualified as a tax expert, and what follows is by no means tax or (God forbid) legal advice. But consider: There is a metaphysical moment in time when you can declare yourself a *writer,* and as I understand it, you have four years after that to show a profit to the government. As a *writer,* you are no longer merely a wage earner with withholding tax and Social Security already taken out of your salary but an entrepreneur, a conductor of your own small business, a person to whom deductions mean everything.

Well, this is just the absolute last *straw,* isn't it? Pick up a book on the literary life and pretty soon I'm lecturing you on your *income tax* when one of the main reasons you wanted to be a writer in the first place was so you wouldn't have to think about things like income tax ever again. I mean, you used to just pick up the short form at the post office, fill in the blanks, and fairly often the Feds sent you some money back, so what's the problem?

For one thing, the government is getting too much of your money. For another, it isn't any fun. And finally, didn't Ralph Waldo Emerson say: "Money, which represents the prose of life, and which is hardly spoken of in parlors without an apology, is, in its effects and laws, as beautiful as roses"?

One thing that the Universe and American tax law have in common is that they slight the dilettante and reward the focused. The dilettante, the absentminded, bored-to-death human files the short form—probably late—and pays through the nose regardless of his or her tax bracket. The genius, the wildly dedicated writer (or artist or even businessman) says: "Oh my God! My *life* is dedicated to writing [or selling potted plants, or surfboards]. The whole country supports me in my industry and enterprise, allowing me all these absolutely fascinating deductions. Fun with the tax man—*yeah!* I'm ready for it!"

Many of you, from entrepreneurial backgrounds, will say, *Duh,* of *course* everybody knows that it's better to structure your life around a business enterprise in which you can take deductions. But the kind of people I was raised around were so prissy about money that it was never mentioned. The idea of deductions was vaguely disgusting, common, venal. Besides, they didn't know how to do it. Women, in particular, even these days, maintain an astonishing level of innocence and ignorance about money, as do the working poor, adolescents, and feckless bachelors. Only when we marry and settle down do we give money much of a thought, and then we tend to run up credit-card debt and suffer greatly.

When I was a penniless divorcée, God, or the Universe, was kind enough to send me to a genius tax lady. She looked like Mary Poppins and sat in the back room of a wacky little shop full of painted dinner plates, fuzzy stuffed kittens, salted nuts, and toys.

Rather than lecturing her women clients on the advantages of having their own business, she showed us *her* extra businesses: the fuzzy kittens, the painted plates. If you have your own business, almost all things are financially possible in this country.

She was such a whiz that you saw well-groomed magnates

in three-thousand-dollar suits, leather briefcases on their laps, crouched among the kitty cats, waiting for Eva to put their affairs in order. And she did. It's *fun,* she said. It has absolutely nothing to do with cheating the government. In fact, she once summarily kicked a would-be cheater out of her office. In her mind, cheating on your taxes was like cheating at golf. The great thing was the *game* and the fun you could have with it. Outside of the very, very wealthy, she used to say, the economics of American life are set up to favor the individual entrepreneur. So why not take advantage of that?

Take the position that you're a writer and a solid citizen. You know, of course, that if you've bought a house, your interest is deductible and your property tax is deductible. Just for the heck of it, your safe-deposit box is deductible. Also your tax man's services. Again, I'm not an authority; check with your tax man, but I understand that thanks to a landmark case fought by Arthur Miller long ago, as a writer, your travel is deductible, because you might write about that travel someday. If you're making those phone calls that make your hands sweat, a portion of your phone bill is deductible. The stationery for your charming notes and the postage? Deductible! Books? Sure! You need them for your calling in life, your "business" of writing. And magazines. And fees for writing conferences. If you hang around with writers and people who support your work, then a portion of your entertaining expenses—when you have your pals over for dinner and take pictures to record the moment and write down your memories of it—part of all the expenses that might accrue from this—is deductible.

Oh, it's fun! If you have to drive for miles on journalism assignments, a portion of your car expenses is deductible. Just write stuff down, keep the receipts, throw them in a box, then tally them up for the tax person. When you hire an agent or a lawyer, their fees may be deductible. When you buy copies of your book, that's deductible. Your parties, book signings, all that stuff is—yes, deductible. And since being a writer depends in great part on being on good terms with the Universe, you need to remember that charitable giving is deductible. Whether it's a good chunk of money or just a little, every bit that you give away makes you demonstrably richer, and puts you in a better position with God *and* the tax man.

Your computer, your pens, filing cabinets, paper—the more money you spend on all these things, the less money the government gets to spend on its missile programs. And the more money you get to spend on what *you* like, money "as beautiful, in its effects and laws, as roses."

—

That's it. Unless you sell work to the movies or a rich relative dies or you marry a wealthy person, these are the three ways, as I see it, to make some money, to make ends meet. Don't discount the other stuff: They *could* happen. I once sold something to the movies for a *lot* of money. And a sweet old boyfriend died and left me a building. And Hemingway, Mr. Literary/Melancholy himself, made sure to marry only well-to-do women. But in the long run, over the years, in thick times and thin, your writing income—that especially precious brand of currency—can be fattened by applying for grants, working for magazines and newspapers, and looking at April 15 as an opportunity to play a game that completely and legally rewards your creativity: Fun with the Tax Man.

By doing all this, you're living as a writer, creating a literary life inside yourself as well as outside: cajoling the world into letting you do what you love to do and then paying you for it.

Chapter 19

It's a Marriage

Living a literary life is a marriage, and I was never very good at marriage.

During the time I was writing this book—which seemed so easy on the face of it that I was incautious enough to remark "This should be able to write itself"—my life partner of twenty-seven years, John Espey, became desperately sick and then died.

"Anything to keep from writing!" Certainly John's illness seemed a good reason not to write that thousand words a day. Not when I had to take him to the doctor or walk him from one room to another or sit on one end of the couch and watch him sleep at the other as I tried to remember what he'd been like when he was well.

Many days I'd sit out on that balcony I've written about in these pages, and no more than twenty feet away from me, under a bravely pink duvet, John Espey lay dying. ("But at my back I always hear/time's winged chariot hurrying near." No kidding.) For perhaps the first time in my life, I *thought*. I began to worry about the *point:* of writing, of love, of children, of all human activity. Because although I knew people had been dying all along, and though I'd lost my mother this same year, and one of our dearest family friends, I'd never been close to death, the daily process of it, the "thousand words a day" of it. But out of habit, I'd write my own thousand words, about point of view or mailing lists or that phony P.R. lady we made up when we were broke. It was a form of praying, I see now.

As John got worse, I couldn't help but think: What's the *point*? The finest mind and soul I'd ever known was going away. All the writing in the world wasn't going to change that.

For all the reading I'd ever done, there was very little written about death, and the material that existed was pretty inaccurate. There was the religious stuff, plenty of propaganda about "good" and "bad" deaths, and a few flashy doctors of the twentieth century showing off all they know or think they know about how kidneys and livers shut down and how there probably isn't a "soul" at all, but they don't know anything. They didn't know John.

The only writers who seemed to get the drift of death were nineteenth-century English novelists, who caught some of the despair of long illnesses, but they were constrained, by the literary conventions of the day, from mentioning the blood, the urine, the crying out, the falling down, the rest of it. Sometimes—often—when I'd be doing the sixth load of laundry in a day, I'd think of my own grandmother, taking care of her teenage son dying of typhoid, long before I was born. I'd think of all the laundry, the sheets of death. I'd think: *I've never read about any of this.* I'd think about *The Death of Ivan Ilyich.* Who wrote it?—Tolstoy? He was very eloquent about the whole thing, but he left out the blood, the crying in the night, the falling down.

After John died, I took time off from this book to write a sixty-page account of how it had happened and wrote a short letter about it to a couple who had been John's closest friends over the years. After about a month, the wife wrote back: "We were so down after receiving your letter . . ." And the wonderful woman who types my stuff handed back my sixty-page draft with this advice: "You'd at least better get rid of the first five thousand words here, because it makes you sound like a bitch."

You could say that my own relationship with writing and life got pretty attenuated then. Because what is the point of living—or any of its activities—when the setup is: You're going to die and the people you love will die and it will be worse than you can ever imagine! (I'm not saying this is an *original* thought, only that when it hits you, it hits with considerable force.) Every activity—*every* activity—turns out to be just the same: hitting golf balls into little holes or inventing the insulation that goes into airplanes or answering phones at an office. All of it is only killing time until we die.

Writing is one of those activities—no more, no less. All the sacredness and thrill, the bewitching happiness, and the crushing rejections are no more and no less than slicing the ball at the seventeenth hole.

Not only that, I thought, but a good part of the writing

we've been given to read and study is lies. We don't *want* to tell ourselves the truth. Western literature is mostly about heterosexuals intent on breeding or excitable males rushing around some battlefield. (Although I began to see the value of an early, violent death, an altogether understandable impulse to cut to the chase, to die—or kill—and get it over with, because standing exhausted for forty minutes trying to pee is not the human condition at its finest.)

Thoughts like these play hell with your thousand words a day. Because added to the devastating personal question—Who cares?—that bedevils every writer if he or she has an ounce of insight is another question, another answer: What does any of this matter? It's probably all lies anyway, and even if it's the truth as I see it, who's ever going to want to read it or know it?

———

On the other hand, I remember the day I began my first novel—in a slum apartment in what they called Los Angeles's second skid row. We had graduate-school bookshelves all around the room, rough boards singed black with a blowtorch and then scraped with a wire brush to bring out the grain. And since my husband and I were managers of this apartment, we invented a tenant, S. W. Takahashi, enrolled him in several book clubs, and let him order absolutely everything. When the bill collectors became insistent, we just said S.W. had moved on.

In this ratty living room in this slum apartment, surrounded by inviting books, I pulled up to a 1940s dresser that Richard See suggested looked a lot like a desk. I knew to write a thousand words, because that's what Virginia Woolf had talked about in her diaries. The blond wood on the dresser was so *blond,* and the bookshelves so dark, and the handles on the dresser were orange. The paper was yellow, because I'd read somewhere that real writers wrote on yellow sheets . . .

And I started! I wasn't the praying kind then, so I suppose I was talking to myself when I said, "One book. Let me complete just one book, and let it be part of the pile"—I *saw* that pile in my mind's eye, miles high—"of all the books that have ever been written," and I began to write with tears on my face, because at that time the idea of writing meant as much to me as anything in the world.

And then I'd write "She proceeded to eat her hamburger" and would look at that sentence for hours, wondering what was wrong with it, but I still blundered through, because I was crazy in love with the process, insanely happy to begin inventing a world (or trying to), convinced that it was the highest, finest activity known to humankind.

I was warned that I'd lose my family and friends if ever I "told the truth." I was told that men didn't like women who write (and they don't, particularly); but in the afternoons, when my daughter was at nursery school and my husband was out of the house, I'd write. It was as exciting as an affair, directly comparable to a secret love.

At that time, I was absolutely alone as far as writing was concerned. It was just me and Doris Lessing and Saul Bellow and E. M. Forster. In the real world, I was only "an unimportant wife who did not like my life," as Alison Lurie would later write. But I was so entirely enchanted that I didn't even have the voice that said, "Who cares?" It hadn't even kicked in yet. If it had, I suppose I would have answered, "Well, everyone's going to care! How could they *not*?"

I was as arrogant and ignorant and uninformed as the mother of a first baby, who really feels that every other baby born up until now has been just a first draft of *her* baby.

Delusions—of importance, of beauty, of the sacred nature of babies, books, romantic love, soccer games, the newest car, democracy—probably have to come into play for any of us to get anything done. Here's a more realistic take on things: Your baby is quite unattractive; your book has only been written about a thousand times before; you're a wretched soccer player; that car of yours sucks; and democracy is all about bad advertising and corporate rule. Delusion *has* to be in the mix in order for us to get anything done at all. Erasmus called it "folly," but then he praised it.

Literary life is a marriage, not a romance. And, as I said, some of us aren't very good at marriage; the dailiness of it gets us down. The cartoon at the beginning of this chapter isn't meant to be funny—except to people who don't write. ALSO BY THE AUTHOR—oh my goodness! "Out of print, naturally." That would be my first novel, my second, and my third. (Though I console myself by remembering that all of F. Scott Fitzgerald's books were out of print when he died. And that Rod Jones's *Julia Paradise,* one of the finest novels in the language, is out of print in *such* a big way.) "Unadvertised, ignored, and forgotten." I guess that would be *Rhine Maidens.* I loved that book so much, but it was unadvertised, ignored, and forgotten. "Why did I bother?" Each time I look at this picture, I have to smile—at the guy clutching his brow and at the book, entitled *Why Did I Bother?*, with a guy on the cover clutching his brow, and so on. *Making History*—man! Why did I bother? I thought it was so hot that it would change the nature of the world. I love that book, but why did I bother? "The Book with the Lousy Cover"! That would be the German paperback of *The Handyman;* but it wasn't as lousy as the cover of the mass market paperback of *Mothers, Daughters.* I know I should have a sense of humor about these things, but it's hard. "No one bought *this* one, either." Oh God. I guess that would be all of them.

And yet here I am writing a book again, actually thinking that this little set of essays may change some lives, make the writing life a little easier and more fun for some people. And cherishing the thought that American literature belongs to *all* Americans.

It's a marriage, not a romance: the tension of "being in love" and at the same time, somewhere in there, profoundly not giving a shit—but still taking it on faith that you must be in love. And you're counting on that feeling to last for the rest of your life.

Not giving a shit. My father, the pornographer who composed elaborate male fantasies full of genuine passion and wit, also wrote a column for his neighborhood newspaper. He wrote that recipe for 18-hour chili. Among his other musings, he once typed this sentence: "He felt no more desire for her than a man would for his wife on a hot day." I know I have a Cassandra streak, but that sentence filled me with fear: that you may have been in love once but maybe, after all, you don't give a shit.

You turn your head away from your spouse during those

moments when you're out of love. But you can't look away from the blank page or, more significantly, from pages and pages of a bad first draft.

It's not that you don't remember that you were in love but that you can't feel it—it's gone; it's like looking at your wife on a hot day.

The world isn't glistening, waiting in radiance for you to finish your wonderful book. Probably, it never was.

Oh well!

At one point after John Espey and I had been together about fifteen years, we realized that in California we might possibly be "married" by common law, and only half jokingly considered going out of the country to renew our visas, so to speak, to stay definitively out of marriage.

But how about taking your manuscript to Kinko's on a hot day and the clerk looks at it and says, unenthusiastically, "How many copies?" Or your printer breaks down. Or you're addressing envelopes for those infernal book signings and thinking, Stephen King doesn't have to do this! Or your publisher sends you the invitations they've done up for your party, and somebody somewhere thought it would be a good idea to have a clerk in the basement crank them out on red construction paper.

Or you write two thousand words for a magazine and some woman with the mind of a zit says, "We really wanted this to be more of a personal piece/less of a personal piece. I'm not entirely comfortable with the lead paragraph/the last two paragraphs. The middle seems too long to us/how about cutting it by about two-thirds? There's no story here/we think you need to get more quotes . . ."

Yesterday, I had lunch with a nonfiction writer who'd made a lunch date in New York with her editor, waited for her for an hour, then left in a rage, only to see that same editor at a table for two, having lunch with a whole other writer.

And then you come home, pick up your writing, find the phrase "He threw back his head and laughed" three times on the very same page.

I ask you: *Why did I bother?* Why *do* I bother?

Because a year or two ago my Slovak sainted second ex-husband, Tom, came over for a dinner party at my daughter Lisa's house, which included his grown daughter from another marriage, our daughter Clara from our own marriage, and a hapless bachelor, son of Tom's best friend, dead from hard living. One way or another, the kids ganged up on Tom, an old guy now, who might have had too much to drink. But he, mulish, balked. He wasn't going to say anything against any of these "children" *or* his ex-wives *or* his dead friend, and he wasn't going to get mad, either. He sat there and the light changed and his hair began to glow and there were his cheekbones and his whole beautiful obdurateness appeared and I had to think, or say, Quit picking on him! Because, it goes without saying, I still loved him.

And just after my mother died, I saw my first husband, Richard, at a book signing of Lisa's and he said, "Sorry about your mom." Then he fell back against a stucco wall, laughing. He laughed so hard his knees buckled, and then he said again, "Sorry," went on laughing until he got tears in his eyes, but not from grief. And I thought, Thank God for Richard. He knows the truth from a pack of lies.

Now, after John has died, I have to remember how much I

loved him. We really were together for better or worse and in sickness and in health till death did us part. In spite of our best efforts, our "romance" turned out to be a marriage.

I have to say—self-absorbed or not—that there are sentences of my own I love so much I quote them to myself: "Loraine made every moment the beginning of a myth," or, "Venice is flat, is still," or, "Dead people, drowned people, have pearls for their eyes." Maybe the world wasn't waiting in radiance for me to write those sentences, but maybe *I was*. Maybe it wasn't other people's loneliness I was striving to alleviate but my own. And maybe I did. If you love this stuff, this writing, it's worth your best effort, worth as much as the dizziest romance or the stormiest divorce or the most enduring marriage.

Since John has died, I live alone. Like most people who live alone, I've taken to talking to myself—not to excess, I hope. But I've tried to notice what it is I generally say.

"I don't know" is what I generally say. Or, "Well, *I* don't know!" But then I also hear myself saying, so often that it surprises me, "Well, we had some fun."

I don't think life is over; that's not it. What I mean is, my life has been fun, not a vale of tears at all, mostly because of the writing. If you can stand the dailiness of it—the continuing marriage of your inner life to all the confusion of the outside world—you can have some *fun!*—in the very highest and most profound sense.

Now, there will be those who say the publishing world has gone to hell in a handbasket, that the book—especially the "literary novel"—is dying, that magazines are expiring, that it's impossible to make a living as a writer, that nobody reads anymore, that the American public can't figure out anything more complicated than a video game, that if you do tell the truth about what you know, you'll lose all your friends and family, eke out a miserable living on unemployment, and die unloved. Your family won't even pick you up from the morgue.

But, again, to quote myself (and why not?—that's part of the fun of being a writer), "I heard most of those stories, and I don't think much of them. I'm telling you, don't believe those other guys. Believe me."

Because we live in a beautiful, sentient universe that yearns for you to tell the truth about it. If you love this world and this craft, they will lift you to a place you can't begin to imagine.

Acknowledgments

First, I must thank all my students over the years, always "so various, so beautiful, so new." I love them more than I can say.

This book was written in a period of hard times for me, and I'm not sure I could have done it without the stalwarts of the Women's Lunch Group: Linda Phillips, Susan Chehak, Jo Giese, Rae Lewis, Luchita Mullican, Virginia Mullin, Maria Munroe, Doreen Nelson, Amanda Pope, Judith Searle, Janet Sternburg, and Susan Suntree. Also, thanks to Jeanette Griver and Patty Seidenbaum for extraordinary friendship in a real time of need.

Many thanks to the people at Medway Plantation for their marvelous generosity: to Joel Conarroe for recommending me, to Bokara Legendre for her generosity and inspiration, and to Oneathea Rogers, Doris Walters, and Robert Hartman, all of them graciousness personified.

Much gratitude to my agent, Anne Sibbald; editor, Lee Boudreaux; copy editor, Veronica Windholz; and friends Linda de Martinez and Ase Karlson. All of them radiant beings!

I owe everything to my "overextended family": Richard See, Tom Sturak, Bob Laws, Lynda Laws, Susan Espey, Jordan and Katrina Espey, Lisa See Kendall, Alexander Kendall, Christopher Kendall, Richard Kendall, Chris Chandler, and Dash Chandler.

But my special thanks go out to Clara Sturak, who was guardian angel to this project, and to the memory of John Espey, who, in Clara's words, "taught us to be civilized. No yelling in the house; keep food in the refrigerator and money in your pockets."

I love you.

Reading List

Isabel Allende, *The House of Spirits*
Kay Boyle, *Fifty Stories*
Michael Chabon, *Wonder Boys*
Gregg Easterbrook, *This Magic Moment*
James Ellroy, *Black Dahlia*
C. S. Forester, *Beat to Quarters*
E. M. Forster, *A Room with a View*
————, *The Longest Journey*
William Gibson, *Neuromancer*
Ernest Hemingway, *The Sun Also Rises*
————, "The Short Happy Life
of Francis Macomber," from
*The Complete Stories of Ernest
Hemingway*
Frank Herbert, *Dune*
Carl Hiaasen, *Native Tongue*
Henry James, *The Ambassadors*
Kay Redfield Jameson, *An Unquiet Mind*
Jon Krakauer, *Into Thin Air*
Anne Lamott, *Rosie*
————, *Bird by Bird*

Elmore Leonard, *Cuba Libre*
————, *Touch*
James McBride, *The Color of Water*
Iris Murdoch, *Under the Net*
Annie Proulx, *The Shipping News*
Carolyn See, *Golden Days*
Art Spiegelman, *The Complete Maus*
Rose Tremain, *The Way I Found Her*
Don Westlake, any of the Dortmunder books
Tim Winton, *Cloudstreet*
Paramahansa Yogananda, *Autobiography of a Yogi*

ABOUT THE AUTHOR

CAROLYN SEE, the author of nine books, has won both a Guggenheim and a Getty Fellowship and has served on the boards of the Modern Library, the National Book Critics Circle, and PEN Center USA West. She teaches English at UCLA and is Friday-morning book reviewer for *The Washington Post*. She lives in Pacific Palisades, California. She can be reached at csee@ucla.edu, and you can visit her Web site: www.carolynsee.com.

ABOUT THE TYPE

This book was set in Sabon, a typeface designed by the well-known German typographer Jan Tschichold (1902–74). Sabon's design is based upon the original letter forms of Claude Garamond and was created specifically to be used for three sources: foundry type for hand composition, Linotype, and Monotype. Tschichold named his typeface for the famous Frankfurt typefounder Jacques Sabon, who died in 1580.